NOTES FROM A SPIRIT BABY MEDIUM

Everything You Need to Know About Spirit Baby Communication

Kelly Ann Meehan, MA

Spirit Baby Inc. Publishing

Topanga, California

Notes from a Spirit Baby Medium

©Kelly Ann Meehan, 2024

Spirit Baby Inc.

Visit Author's Website: www.newearthchildren.com

Email: spiritbabymedium@gmail.com

All rights reserved. No part of this book may be used or reproduced by any means, graphic, electronic, or mechanical, including photocopying, recording, taping, or by any information retrieval storage system, without the written permission of the author, except in the case of brief quotations embodied in critical articles or reviews.

ISBN: 979-8-9913510-0-3

For privacy reasons, some names may have been changed.

Disclaimer: The content of this book is for informational purposes only and is not intended to diagnose, treat, cure, or prevent any condition or disease. You understand that this book is not intended as a substitute for consultation with a licensed practitioner. Please consult with your own physician or healthcare specialist. The use of this book implies your acceptance of this disclaimer.

Please note that the author doesn't make any guarantees about the results of the information applied in *Notes from a Spirit Baby Medium*. The publisher does not claim to have all the answers. It is best to always trust and discern based on your intuition and gut instincts. If something you read sits wrong, then use it as a healing tool and take action on what you need. There are no absolutes within spiritual knowledge, only experiences and explorations through personal discovery, self-education, and Ascension.

Edited by Robin Quinn / www.writingandediting.biz

Book design by – PapaLeoArts

NOTE TO READER

This book can be a spiritual guide for parents-to-be, parents, birth professionals, midwives, doulas, therapists, counselors, healers, as well as fertility and pregnancy coaches. It is for those who want to bring a new evolved understanding to how we conceive through the physical, energetic, emotional, and spiritual self with spirit baby communication and soul awareness. This work is meant to teach new self-awareness, self-inquiry, mindful reflections, and self-healing.

DEDICATION

My book is dedicated to all the amazing spirit baby seekers, heart communicators, world-changing visionaries, and the futurists who are on a mission to protect and guide our New Earth Children. We are in a time of eminent change and heart healing fellowship. We must welcome remembrance into a deeply gentle and natural way towards conception into birth; For it is critical to preserve nature for the next generation for the children and for all of humanity.

CONTENTS

ACKNOWLEDGMENTS vii

FOREWORD ix

PREFACE xv

INTRODUCTION xxi

CHAPTER ONE 1
    Spirit Baby Communication 101 1

CHAPTER TWO 25
    Messages from Spirit Baby 25

CHAPTER THREE 43
    Intuition and Spirit Baby Communication 43

CHAPTER FOUR 57
    The Art of Spirit Baby Communication, Part 1 & An Introduction to the New Children of the Earth 57

CHAPTER FIVE 67
    The Art of Spirit Baby Communication, Part 2 (More Tools) .. 67

CHAPTER SIX 89
    Conscious Conception – A Star Is Welcomed 89

CHAPTER SEVEN 101
    Infertility – Surrendering Into Healing 101

CHAPTER EIGHT 119

    Pregnancy – A Pre-Birth Communication Experience 119

CHAPTER NINE 145

    Miscarriage – The Afterlife of Spirit Baby - 1 145

CHAPTER TEN 163

    Still Birth/Infancy Death – The Afterlife of Spirit Baby - 2 163

CHAPTER ELEVEN 177

    Abortion – Releasing Pregnancy and Heart Healing 177

CHAPTER TWELVE 189

    Newborn Spiritual Care – Parenthood after Spirit Baby Communication 189

CONCLUSION 197

REFERENCES 199

ABOUT THE AUTHOR 201

ACKNOWLEDGMENTS

Most of all, my heart and gratitude goes to my husband, my best friend, and my soulmate, Rene, for always supporting me in all my creative projects, listening to my spiritual rants, and holding my deeper vision in serving others. I have always felt held and positively guided in dreaming my ideas into reality with Rene by my side.

To my hearts running around free outside of me...my boys Rain and Forest for bringing love and motherhood into my life. My children have made this book possible on so many levels of who I am and continue to become. I am opened up by motherhood. It has reshaped and brought purpose into my life that keeps inspiring and healing as a daily prayer and a spiritual mantra.

More thanks goes to my supportive soul sister, my bestie Wendy. Who has been an inspiration and always motivating in her kind and loving support, And to my star-soul family for the support and love: Tristan, Heidi, Saoirse, and my healers Nancy and Emily, and all the others that I have connected with throughout the years that inspire me to show up with heart!

FOREWORD

Over the years, I have always been fascinated whenever I heard Kelly speak about her amazing experiences as a spirit baby medium. Now, with her first book, she has taken another major step to assist in making a much needed paradigm shift on the planet about the value and significance of her field of expertise, *spirit baby communication.*

Kelly's experiences in the field of *spirit baby communications* teach us that babies even before conception share with us the mysterious gift of human consciousness. Contrary to what we have been taught for more than 100 years, the baby's sentience, sense of self, and diverse capabilities are not dependent on brain development. They precede it.

The baby's primary nature is a conscious, sentient, non-physical being who exists prior to and beyond physical human existence. Basically, because the prevailing view in psychology and medicine doesn't acknowledge this, babies have been treated as merely biological bodies without a sentient soul from conception to birth.

Scientists who define a baby as physical matter say that a baby's brain matter is insufficient to register or process memory, learning, trauma, emotion, or any human experiences until months after birth. False ideas about the brain are the justification for cruel and abusive treatment. However, research shows that babies can feel pain even *in utero*. Clinical reports in Pre-and Perinatal Psychology reveal unfortunate-to-tragic effects when interventions are carried out while ignoring the baby's sentient nature. Babies are far more advanced Beings than outdated medical theory pretends.

Kelly's book lends support to eliminating medically-caused pain on the baby's journey to birth. Providers of physical care should consider the effect of a procedure on the baby's emotions and mind. Babies are affected by their interactions with others and are learning from their experiences from the beginning of life.

Like Kelly, I too have a strong interest in this topic. The journey of our soul to earthly life first captured my attention in 1989 in researching the topic "Are there mothers who give birth without pain?" In my interviews with mothers, they quickly expanded the topic with countless experiences in their journey to motherhood beginning with the preconception stage.

Mothers described profound encounters with babies not yet conceived. They shared dreams, visions, and other vivid events in which a future baby announced its coming, and brought love, encouragement, and guidance to mother and father.

As an example, Nan described spirit baby communications with her son:

> *During my pregnancy with Paul, he got me out of a pattern of blindly following the advice men gave me. When my doctor told me, "Oh, that is normal. No need to worry about it," Paul would call him on it, "Mom, don't listen to the doctor. You know better than that."*
>
> *Another time, the doctor prescribed white tablets for morning sickness. The message I received from my son*

was: "Mom, don't take these pills. They cause birth defects."

Within a few years, research proved that those pills caused birth defects. I am happy that I listened. Paul's destiny was to have a healthy body.

Another sign of the advanced nature of babies, as described in our book, *Babies Are Cosmic, Signs of Their Secret Intelligence,* is that babies in the womb seem to perceive what their mothers and fathers are feeling and saying about them. For example, babies know if they are wanted or unwanted—a perception reflected in elevated risk of death in the first 28 days of life between wanted and unwanted babies.

In our book, *Cosmic Cradle, Spiritual Dimensions of Life before Birth*, we report the case of Summer's spirit baby communications when she became unexpectedly pregnant with a second child. Following Summer's earnest prenatal dialog describing to the incoming child why the pregnancy was untimely and requesting the baby to come back when certain conditions were fulfilled in Summer's life, Summer experienced a spontaneous miscarriage the next day. This experience among others is further evidence of precocious understanding on the part of babies before birth. Summer's daughter did come back a year later when the 3 conditions Summer requested in her spirit for baby communication had been fulfilled making it a more appropriate time to bring another child into the family.

Another sign of the conscious baby before birth are pre-birth memories or pre-conception memories. Pre-birth memories of adults and children often reflect that their primary nature is spiritual prior to entering human lives. They associate their real sense of home to the spirit realm, not the earthly human plane. Many recall choosing parents and of transcendental perception.

As an example, author Elisabeth Hallett, a pioneer in the field of life before birth, gathered accounts of pre-birth communication and pre-birth memories. One example is a conversation with her 3-year-old son Devin:

> *We were sitting together on the back porch of our home when he suddenly said, "Mommy, let's go home."*
>
> *"Where's our home?"*
>
> *"Far, far away," said Devin.*
>
> *Pointing upward, he went on: "Up in the sky. This is a dirt place. Our home is up there."*

Children's pre-birth memories, like Devin's, reveal a sense of self prior to incarnation that is capable of communicating with future parents in the physical world.

Babies before birth are much more than we thought. And Kelly's new book supports a deep understanding about who babies really are—even before conception. Kelly aligns with findings from experimental research, Pre- and Perinatal Psychology, Psychotherapy, and anecdotal reports which render traditional views of human development obsolete.

This more complex consciousness demands a new standard of medical care that includes the power of love.

Elizabeth Carman, MSCI, PhD (H), PPNE

Leading author along with Neil Carman, PhD, of *Cosmic Cradle, Spiritual Dimensions of Life Before Birth; Babies Are Cosmic, Signs of Their Secret Intelligence.*

PREFACE

My Beginnings with Spirit Baby Communication

My first experience with spirit baby communication came when I was in graduate school in the depths of my Clinical Psychology program with an emphasis in Somatic Psychology. The year was 2005. The program offered a Prenatal and Perinatal Psychology emphasis as well, and I was able to experience some of that education through crossover classes. This was how I first learned about Birth Psychology. I was so fascinated by Somatic Psychology and focused on that program the most. I enjoyed learning about my body-mind connection in a body-mind psychology format. It was a life-changing experience to be a student at the Santa Barbara Graduate Institute (SBGI), located in Santa Barbara, California. I was able to learn from the most incredible master expert teachers in the fields of Somatic Psychology and Prenatal and Perinatal Psychology. I learned a little bit about everything: Somatic Experiencing, Hakomi Therapy, Sensory Awareness, Gestalt, Body-Mind Psychotherapy, Bodynamics Analysis, Postural Integration, Neuroscience, and so much more. I had teachers such as Judyth Weaver, Susan Aposhyan, Aline LaPierre, JoAnne Chartrand-Benz, Syrian Benz-Chartrand, and others. Honestly, it was an incredible experience with higher educational teaching and advanced embodiment skill building and healing. I will forever be grateful for it and keep learning through other programs such as SmartBody SmartMind

(SBSM) with Irene Lyon and other new endeavors such as Trauma Resolution Exercise (TRE).

Back to my story. During lunch, the students would gather often in the local park across the street from the children's big playground. The park was a beautiful place in Santa Barbara. It had a pond always full of turtles, a maintained walking path, bridges to connect to other areas of the park, and water canals. The park was not too far from the coast of the Pacific Ocean, so you could smell and feel the dampness and salt in the air.

One sunny day with bright blue skies, many of us got together on the hillside of the park. After a nice lunch, we engaged in conversation. Soon we ended up offering a loving energy healing touch to our classmate and friend, who was seven months pregnant. Our pregnant classmate allowed Reiki, energy healing, and other loving touch modalities for her and her baby. Everyone was sending love and good vibes to her for pregnancy into birth.

As the mama-to-be classmate lay on the earth, I remember sitting above her shoulders on the grass. That is when I saw her babies. I saw a boy and a girl. I saw them within my mind and felt their presence. I sensed them as if the two stood right next to her and they appeared as pre-school-aged children. I shared with everyone aloud that I saw twin children and it was a boy and a girl. I asked my pregnant classmate if she was having two babies. She said no. The mother-to-be assured me that she was having a boy because she felt it. She did no medical interventions or sonogram and her midwifery care was supportive of this. Close to thirty-eight weeks, she gave birth at home to her boy first, and second, her daughter would follow. She had twins! That is when I realized that this was more than my imagination. I continued to explore my communication with others in pregnancy whenever it came up to see what babies wanted to share and how it all worked.

I could "hear" babies in spirit because I was listening, I guess, or some higher calling unfolded to my surprise. This was not something I had ever heard or read about until I found the book *Spirit Babies* by Walter Makichen. His book is like a "bible" for this specific energy of spirit babies. I would not call myself a "Spirit Baby Medium" until many years later, starting with the term "Pre-Birth Communicator" in 2012. I was always trying to figure out what I do and how to explain it. So Spirit Baby Medium eventually came to me and this was a title that stuck. I then feverishly searched the Internet for the meaning of the term and nothing existed. I have defined Spirit Baby Medium as someone who can communicate and connect with a baby before conception, in the womb during pregnancy, and after life in death. It involves being a messenger and offering a specific vibration that connects through intuitive spiritual skills and psychic awareness with children in spirit.

Thereafter, I have supported thousands of women and men with spirit baby communication messages, medical intuitive scans, somatic embodiment, grief healing apprenticeship, and healing mentorship within private one-on-one sessions, online programs, groups, pop-in workshops, monthly memberships, and free listening support through my podcast and other events. Plus, the deck *Spirit Baby Oracle: Soul Answers from Spirit Baby* spirituality-at-home deck for spirit baby communication practices. Future muses include poetry with spirit baby and a spirit baby notebook for journaling with thought provoking questions to explore. In addition, The Spirit Baby Academy is a six-month certification for students to focus and learn spirit baby communication to work with others as healers, therapists, couches, doulas, midwives, holistic practitioners, psychologists, and doctors.

Additional Love Message for You

Parenting is a spiritual journey. That is a fact. In one's life, it is very significant. I want you to experience how you can find your own support through it. This is not meant to be a lonely undertaking. I know we all have special gifts and talents to offer in these powerful times on Earth. I was born into heightened sensitivities and I accept that. I have built my heart's reality around it, not entirely without fear. But I work on weaving in more and more loving confidence and radiance. I am like a "rememberer" and that means I am here to remind you to remember your greatest potential and achievability within creation. To promote your own creation within yourself through the earthmind, but more inside the space of timelessness and accessing the truest vibrations of how conception and pregnancy into birth support you.

I am speaking to you directly. Please do not overthink what you are receiving. Instead, be playful and laugh with joy as you learn about yourself and how you communicate and sense spirit babies or babies. Feel it and sense it. I want you to sit with your heart and let your mind be passive at times to take up the spaces in your background. Let your mind be free and without the main focus or holding expectations. I actually want to encourage you to move into questioning, surrendering, embodiment, and a state of being self-judgment free. To allow any resistance or fears that come up to be observed and not battled. For you to normalize any negative or uneasy or unsure thought or experience. I want you to look deeply through all corners of your spiritual self in order to receive your wholeness and love.

So take a breath and give yourself some love, because the energy of spirit baby is a language of energy and spirit baby communication that you have access to naturally. I am going to help you get to it and become an expert. I want you to remember this book is here to support you, to help you access your personal skill-building abilities, to push you, to activate you, to assist you in letting go, to love you through it, and to be your best reminder of the strength of your own heart.

Keep opening up to the experience without limitations by anyone or anything. Explore your infinite possibilities and your deeper self by trusting your intuition. All of this will help connect you to spirit baby communication during your personal voyage into motherhood and beyond.

INTRODUCTION

It Could Be Best to Start at the Start

Babies are born around the world every minute, coming into certain genetics, lineages, races, cultures, socioeconomic statuses, and more. UNICEF, a humanitarian organization for helping children and adolescents, estimates that an average of 140 million babies are born each year globally.

I want you to pause and take that in. Involve yourself in a compelling reflection on how many little human beings are coming to Earth every single day. We should be celebrating a birthday every day. These little beings come with a purpose and some unknown agreement to experience many lessons, and also to teach us and guide us daily and into the future.

You are going to learn all about that here!

Earth is undergoing some kind of re-birthing process. Parts of our planet are thriving, and inside the cycles of life, we see re-birth through life and through death. Earth is changing. Meanwhile, humans are just like Earth and a part of it more than many realize. Our consciousness is changing, and it is not about thinking, over-figuring it out, or solving it. The change is innate and many can sense it and feel it. I know we are on a massive shift upon our planet. We are witnessing it happening around us through social media and new technologies like AI, and continuous human and Earth changes. Earth knows what it needs in this reboot or metamorphosis. Humanity is also ready because there are no other choices. We are all in creation holding heart-responsibilities as active Divine and cosmic participants to something truly amazing, miraculous, intense, and altering.

We all understand that life begins in the uterus or the womb. The womb is a most precious space of gestation and a portal that gives birth to humanity. Whether there is natural conception or in-vitro fertilization, the womb needs a certain environment to bring a baby into a bodily existence with certain nutrients and special nourishment for development, and more.

Basic biology comes together through cell formation, building organs and more, because that is nature. Yet this glorious and gorgeous vessel or body cannot exist without a soul or spirit. Don't you agree? I will share more about soul and spirit in Chapter 1, and how the spirit arrives in the before-birth world to greet her or his body. The soul holds a sacred intelligence and a multidimensional truth. Trust and the purity of love already know how to naturally exist within babies, and all you need to do is open with ease and connection to join the miracle and magic. This is a baby.

Conception Is Nature

Let's look deeper at the biology involved here. Biology and science help us explore and understand life and our world. Our life has been built upon many different theories, ideas, experiments, and study, especially within conception and child development. It has been shared that conception looks similar to patterns and natural shapes of nature. It is through the creation of spirals, waves, lights, reflections, cycles, like that seen in leaves, waters, mountains, and more. The egg and sperm merge in human union with a spark of light and this has been captured in video and pictures. Through historical observation and learning, it has been witnessed. We know uninterrupted conception naturally forms, just like nature intended. The form takes on a geometric pattern by coming together organically. It is the start of a zygote, which becomes an embryo and gestates into a fetus and later is birthed as an infant into life.

I guess you can say that conception is like a math equation or formula, and it has its own language. It literally has been seen to glow in its own creative forms. The beautiful mystery and the phenomena of conception will always be dissected, studied, and researched because people need to try to figure it out. That is how science works in the mind. As societies expand and welcome a new consciousness with high intuitive intellect, then more realizations of science and spirit can and will be offered and revealed. Advanced ways will arrive soon, not just AI technologies, but other spiritual wonders.

Ancient Ways Beyond Science

Science is just a small part of conception and pregnancy that warrants tribute and respect, and it is not everything. We need to be careful with this belief that science has all the answers because we need to know everything. It is so much more than needing to have the right answers or data. Science cannot save us or make us feel cozy inside all the time. More is happening that science can not keep up with. In order to best fit within the new developing knowledge of Parapsychology, Metaphysics, Quantum Mechanics, and Epigenetics, we need to let each be their own study of information, be an authority in that area and experience it for what value each holds.

Humans are *spirits first* living as biological beings, with the ability to access high levels of consciousness that go beyond the basics of thinking, reasoning, solving, and creating. This includes beliefs and cultural traditions about conception within ancient native and indigenous traditions passed on throughout history in certain regions around the world. Religious, spiritual, and earth-based practices are what give meaning to many people, providing beliefs for guidance and purpose.

Many believe in some kind of Divinity like God or the Feminine Goddess, but you do not need to embrace that to be in spirit baby communication. You can be an agnostic or an atheist. Spirit baby communication goes beyond religion. It is for everyone, regardless, because it is a natural instinct to create a baby. It is love. It is life. It is a miracle.

Spirit baby communication relates to sacred practices that many indigenous cultures already understand. They engage in ritual and ceremony as an invitation for the "spirit child," and share knowledge from ancestors. For example, anthropological exploration within the Australian aboriginal traditions believes in "dreaming" about a "spirit child" before they enter into the family. Spirit baby consciousness could be the next movement into teachings of past times of connection, intuition, and creation with life. Humans will continue to discover more about themselves and more about conception into pregnancy. In the perfection of new levels of Science, humanity will add to this history of tradition. Sharing different cultural stories with the next generations allows nature and the unfolding of life to come together for families and communities.

The New Earth Children

What I can say is that... Humanity is changing. I am not the only one who is experiencing this. It is very profound to be in these times of post-pandemic living. Our current and future children are going to change the world because it is time. We are ready to jump into deeper preservation and protection through maternity care and the prevention and ending of child trafficking. The love of our future humans counts on it! No longer will be the days of suffering. I envision the elimination of abuse, violence, and addictions for the whole of everyone. The change is here and bringing forth speaking up, fighting corruption, modifying old outdated systems, aligning with advocacy, and showing up with a high vibrational community that supports a better way of living and thriving.

The New Earth Children are best being raised differently because they will not tolerate the old ways of falsehood or lies. The New Earth Children are karma-free, with a balanced sensitivity, held by unconditional love, and system busters, lobbying peacekeepers, and more to heal the planet. New Earth Children have a written agreement that is encoded into their body and spirit made of light and wisdom. These children flourish being born naturally with little to no interventions if possible, along with being raised with healthy attachment parenting, in nontoxic environments that have clean water and non-GMO healthy foods. They prosper with freedom in healthy and stress-free living within a holistic model of care and wellness, and more. Our children deserve to have a healthy and carefree life without the enslavement of old ways held by generational traumas. It is a time of the New Earth Energies to be in unconditional love, heart-held authenticity, with the highest vibes of harmony and peace.

I understand that our New Earth Children may not be so easily met by all that I stated, but I do not believe that babies being born are coming seeking perfection or a life of pain and suffering either. Babies want to be born into different life experiences and deeper teachings that unfold through it. All kinds of babies within their magnificent souls will find their way to Earth when it is the most aligned. Babies are meant to be born and they will. Not all babies are meant for Earth life, and it is a hard true experience that some babies will die.

The chapters ahead are focused on the mother-baby relationship, but not to leave out the father-baby relationship. I want to share that babies will not all be the same or come into creation through women- and-men-only partnerships. I want to share neutrality on this hot topic because spirit babies are looking to join all types of families to grow and love. This includes lesbian, gay, bisexual, and/or transgender (LGBTQ) parents, and it is never just about the parents, but the spirit of the relationship being built and agreed upon before life and into life.There is a common belief through the New Age and spiritual beliefs and writings that we choose our life plan before we are born. I cannot confirm nor deny that, but I do know we are here by choice. I also want to leave it up to you to explore.

You Are Ready for Motherhood and It Is Meant to Be...

The heart of a mother has a way that calls in the unborn from a daydream or a nighttime dream. Some call through the prayers or chants whispered within to a higher power or to the self as a declaration of devotion and love. It can be a longtime dream that began years before the child was ever considered as a daily reality, and other times the dream manifests unexpectedly as a desire or readiness. The hopes and openings to be in synchronicity with life and the rhythms of nature are a strongly held wish and purpose. The bond by the hearts in conception and/or pregnancy is real. Put into action and released into the cosmos, a new baby is then born, and love is shared.

As you read this book, you will experience the changing energy fields within your mind and your heart. I welcome you to explore, experience, expand, and discover more about our New Earth Children and what it means to be a parent for the future through consciously conceiving, creating a spiritual pregnancy, birthing in freedom, and being initiated into motherhood and or fatherhood. You may need to heal after loss through mediumship, if that is your experience. The time may not be right for you and baby. You may be reading this because something calls to you in pre-conception; you want to learn about conscious parenting. Or you may be supporting others in fertility, healing, and pregnancy towards self-trust, self-awareness, and self-love. Whatever it is, welcome and get ready to change your energy and celebrate your new energy agreements.

CHAPTER ONE

Spirit Baby Communication 101

"The universe is giving the earth with souls appropriate for this stage of our development as a species. It is not sending us the kind of souls that were required in the nineteenth century, or the ninth century. It is sending us souls of the twenty-first century, harbingers of the light. Look into the eyes of a newborn baby. There is wisdom there, a connection with universal source that is utterly present."

*~ Dawson Church, **Communing with the Spirit of Your Unborn Child***

The teachings I grew up in told me that when people die or transition we call them a "spirit." They go home to God, go home to Heaven, attain Nirvana, or disappear. I have also heard that we become one with the stars and space dust and/or become one with Universal Energy. Spiritual literature and teachings often speak about the World of the Living and the World of the Dead, but from my experience I have not read or heard much about the World of the Before Life and how we come into being before our bodies. Somehow death experiences and stories with mediumship are more prevalent throughout history and the sharing of it through famous mediums.

Questions I am always asked...

These are common inquiries and questions I have heard and been asked over a decade of supporting spirit baby communication and parents. *What is a spirit baby? What is spirit baby communication? What is a spirit baby medium? How do I communicate with my baby? How do I know I am communicating properly? How do I know it is not wishful thinking or just my imagination?*

I love these questions and I want to answer them all, plus more. I believe we need to support personal curiosity and one's own inner knowledge. It is great to have insights and questions about how you can build a relationship with your spirit baby and apply spirit baby communication into your life through creative practices and accessing your own abundance and spiritual connections.

One thing I know for sure is that spirit babies are real. That communication happens all the time in my life and often even every day. The pre-life or life before life does exist. And, yes, there are ways to communicate with spirit babies, and I am going to share more about the methods that are effective with practice, trust, confidence, and love. I hope for you to gain a new experience and outlook on life through the spiritual connections you make and for you to become an expert in your own heart. I promise that you are not crazy or making it all up, and it is not wishful thinking or fearful or fantasy imagination. You are going to have real experiences to further develop who you are and who you are becoming.

My questions for you...

Are you ready to become a parent? Are you unsure of it? Are you a little bit of both, in feeling ready and unsure about becoming a parent?

I trust that you are in the right place with having many feelings and thoughts about becoming a parent for the first time or second or third. Maybe spirit baby communication is all new to you, or maybe you are already an amateur or pro at having visions or sensing or dreaming with or about spirit babies or babies.

You are in the right place:

- If you are struggling to conceive
- If you have experienced birth loss (single or multiple) within miscarriage, termination, or infancy loss after life and are on a path to heal.
- If you are in pregnancy wanting a spiritual loving bond, needing support and encouragement, or have pregnancy fears or anxiousness.

You are exploring and building energy, whether you are:

- On a preconception path preparing
- Have no idea when to start conceiving
- Unsure of where your future partner is
- Are waiting for both you and your partner to be ready, but need more time
- Are on a solo path as a single parent on purpose or by accident

Your parenthood journey only needs simple things from you. You are opening up to conceive and reflecting on what it means to open up to receive your child into your life. I feel it begins with a heart's agreement with yourself and the child or children you know you are meant to have and desire. So no matter where you are and what is going on, just be open, receive, and listen to what serves the path forward into motherhood and/or fatherhood.

Remember Who You Are and How Spirit Baby Communication Is Guiding You...

You're learning and developing your spirit baby communication awareness, and you are going to build awesome skills that will open you up for a new practice. I invite you to listen to the frequency of your creative self and let your spirit baby or babies guide you. Allow your inner curiosities to offer you change, conception healing into pregnancy, and get your heart space super ready for what comes next.

Yes, get ready. You are meant to activate your spirit baby communication skills with messages that will provide spiritual openings, heighten telepathic psychic senses, and supportive tips and tools. You will be developing your own unique practices from conception communication into pre-birth pregnancy communication.

Don't stress, and just follow the detailed exercises and meditations to get clarity with your spirit baby vibrations. Remember that you can and will connect, and it will be on your own beautiful insightful journey with love and an expansion of heart.

What is a spirit baby?

A spirit baby is a conscious being with a Spirit or a Soul or an Energy. The spirit is an electrifying energy of potential life, and an ultimate essence of deep infinite love and truth. Spirit babies have an availability to be embodied as a human baby upon Earth. The origins of the term "spirit baby" are unknown, but many ancient and modern societies have experienced intuitive realizations about children on their way, in the world of nighttime dreams, and through daydreams of psychic phenomena. There are no hard rules about connecting with your spirit child before life or after. Some simple vocabulary to explore when understanding spirit babies are soul, spirit, spirit baby, baby spirit, child spirit, light child, Spark, Divinity, and child of light, to name some.

The idea of a connection with spirit is an intimate union that lives in the secrets of many minds, and it is a birthright to our becoming ourselves. That means we have information inside us from the start of our own birth into being. This information can easily be ignored or has become buried inside in the subconscious or feared. Yet it is here and ready to be listened to now. A consciously conceiving parent is ready to explore new openings and brings healing into the ever-expanding energies of spirit babies.

The idea or philosophies of spirit babies can be bewildering, but also continuously changing through experiences shared by others that were not set in books until more recently. It can be hard to fully understand with overthinking or disconnection and following societal beliefs. Prepare and get ready for inception with a defined spirit purpose. A spirit baby has its own laid out expedition and for many different known and unknown reasons that you will have to figure out. It is all in sequence to create a deeper sense of self in a bodily experience to call forth spiritual advancement.

There are many experiences and pearls of wisdom about the spiritual philosophy of spirit baby communication, and the evidence is in the people with hundreds into thousands of parents, relatives, and those highly perceptive to awakening to spirit baby experiences and even visiting the spirit baby realms. These experiences with spirit baby communication are within conception, pregnancy, and birth loss. The stories are shared and passed on through words, pictures, and storytelling.

Can you tell me more about spirit baby or soul baby?

I have come to know that the spirit baby or soul baby is the truth of existence. An essence. A purity like no other. It is Love. It is Grace. It is Energy. It is of Soul. It is a potential of life. It exists with a body or without. I do believe it is sacred. It is power. It is creation. It is abundant. It is infinite. You may have heard or felt the same about the spirit baby. There is so much literature that attempts to explain the true meaning of being a soul or spirit. I would consider it a master of its own kind. It is like art or a creative Spark birthed by the light of Source, the Universe, or God. From that birth, a light becomes formed into actuality. This is you. This is Love. This is a baby. This is my poetic experience of what it means to be a spirit or soul.

It is powerful to remember that life is special and everyone born comes with different gifts and adventurous missions that oftentimes get revealed over a lifetime. In my experience of the "Spirit Baby World," there are infinite amounts of soul babies knowing, preparing, and readying to be born upon Earth through a human called "mother" for a way here. That pre-birth space is not sorcery or some kind of voodoo or darkness. I sense it as an infinite space that has no barriers or ordering rules. I imagine it is formless and resistant to any holding. It can be a liminal space or the in-between waiting room before the realm of the Earth School of Life. Words can not and never will adequately describe something that is wordless and only properly beheld by experience.

Let's use your imagination for a moment. Begin by closing your eyes and seeing a vast space like a galaxy of stars inside unlimitedness. Allow that vastness to be filled with lights that twinkle subtly. Those are the little babies full of brightness choosing the appropriate families to join for moments to years. We are born to forget so much to experience new things to be held by our hearts and our family and friends. The before-life preparation may be hard to think about or imagine. But somehow this birthing process brings spirit into body and an exchange happens. A baby is born into a certain body, gender, personality, and appearance, and it is celebrated.

How do you communicate with your baby before life?

Spirit baby communication is not scary, nor does it go against any religion or spiritual practices or require having any spiritual practices. It is instinctual, and it lives within an awareness between parent(s) and child that begins with listening inward, connecting, trusting, and exploring. It is natural and inside you. It is available to everyone. It requires love, presence, patience, and receiving.

Spirit baby communication does not need to be a challenge, and it involves listening and self-awareness that includes internal and external cues. Awareness will lead you towards your personal development with your spirit baby practices. The skills of self-awareness are the most needed, and they will support you and your baby communication. Remember to discover your own way into embodied trust and spiritual attunement within the intuitive and psychic space.

Being truly open will be your best friend, and make it easier to connect to your personal extraordinary abilities. Within your abilities, you can develop how to serve and align yourself lovingly with spirit baby oneness and goodness to have a relationship from conception to pregnancy into birthing.

Remember that communication begins with the parent-to-be and the unique loving force of consciousness within the spirit baby. Your spirit baby communication practices will not be all the same, for each child is different. Communication, from my experience, depends on the parent or parents and the child or children. When you are in agreement with your intuition, then you can be in creation with life and receive, connect, and heal your own heart. In your heart, more healing will come with baby being sharing messages of creativity, healing light, and profound personal growth.

How can I build my spirit baby communication and what encourages my spirit baby communication awareness?

You may have many questions about how and where to begin your spirit baby communication practices. Here are some steps you can take.

STEP 1: Visit and listen to the *Spirit Baby Radio Podcast* at www.newearthchildren.com/spirit-baby-radio. It has episodes to encourage your inward journey with such topics as energy vibration, spirit communication teachings, the psychology of parenthood, mediumship and mysticism, and more. These supportive topics can help you build the energy of a healing connection with yourself and with spirit baby or babies.

SPIRIT BABY RADIO *has been on a mission since 2016 to serve humanity into deepening intuitive intelligence, accessing spiritual knowledge, creating awareness, and strengthening community to hold the hearts of everyone. All with the intention to support our children in the future.*

Spirit Baby Radio *believes humans are awakening more and more and seeking resources to heal and bring autonomy and authenticity for trusted guidance and thriving heart connections. The episodes share real experiences with thousands of women and men seeking inspirational guidance within the energies of Spirit Baby connections in pre-conception, pre-birth communication in pregnancy, and soul communication in birth loss. The conversations will keep sharing their unique philosophy of spirit baby communication insights about the creative forces of life of the unborn, birthing new beings from gestation into birth, owning energy for a highly intuitive pregnancy, sacred ritual and grief awareness, and nature's version of attachment and aligned parenting.*

The goal is to continue to share grounding and other beyond universal musings, that align to real-life experiences from expert speakers who have a love of our babies coupled with passion, dedication, and purpose.

STEP 2: Begin with opening your mind to many possibilities. Open up in new ways so you can understand your multidimensional self and trust your self-guidance. You need to be available to explore how your intuition is already being applied to your everyday life. It is okay to sometimes feel super intuitive with accuracy, while at other times having no awareness of it and being on automatic pilot. How valuable it is to remember that spirit baby speaks to your intuition and trusting communication. This communication may challenge you, especially with mental energies of fear and mind projections of criticism, shame, judgment, and other self-abusive emotions and thoughts. Intuition is explored more in a further chapter to help you get grounded and anchored in your spiritual energy and path.

STEP 3: Explore your psychic awareness or psychic self. Do not be scared of being psychic because it is already a part of your life. You are Supernatural! Or I like to say Supernormal! I am here to tell you how to remember and be with your extra-sensory perceptions with loving practice as your confidence rises. Your psychic awareness can involve many experiences that are visual, telepathic, empathic, auditory, kinesthetic, and energetic. That includes nighttime dreaming and daytime dreaming. Your psychic connection is the #1 only way you can be in communication with your spirit baby.

STEP 4: Spirit baby communication is NOT just meditation. Your communication with your spirit baby relationship will come to you in the best way for your connection. For example: I have heard of spirit babies sharing in many ways to communicate with parents from speaking through their journaling/writing/poetry, music, tones, chants, vibrations, dancing, movement, embodiment practices, art, artistic projects, nature, gardening, walking, and more. I once heard a spirit baby say, "My mom needs to knit." The knitting was not about the project result, but about mommy listening and relaxing to open up with relaxation and gentle focus.

Tools of learning can be guiding, and this is why I created easy-to-use Spirit Baby Oracle Cards with supportive messages for inspiration and guidance of intuition. *Spirit Baby Oracle: Soul Answers from Spirit Baby* (a spiritual deck of cards for conception/pregnancy/birth loss) can be found at www.newearthchildren.com/spirit-baby-oracle-cards. The cards are meant to speak from the perspective of your spirit baby or your daughter or son in conception, pregnancy, and birth loss. The messages are uplifting and loving and guiding. Spirit babies are light, active communicators, and messages will come through to you that are reflected in the card. *The cards are available in the USA and Internationally.*

***The* Spirit Baby Oracle: Soul Answers from Spirit Baby cards** *are a unique healing tool to assist your journey into conception, pregnancy, or healing from birth loss. The intention behind the cards is to help you ask your Baby Being for a message. These messages help to create a connection and a long-term relationship with your baby from conception into birth and after birth and if you have experienced birth loss.*

STEP 5: Get your energy synergistic with spirit baby meditations, activities, books, spiritual groups, healing sessions with spirit baby intuitives, and more.

When you tune into resources, you are telling your energy and the Universe that you are ready and it is happening!

Resources heighten your intuition to bring you listening clarity, open you up to curiosities, and help you become flexible with not knowing, welcoming all kinds of experiences, and so much more.

Here is a BOOK LIST of my favorite and recommended readings that are spirit baby/pre-birth communication specific by researchers, teachers, and healers:

Carman, Elizabeth and Carman, Neil J. *Babies Are Cosmic: Signs of Their Secret Intelligence*

Carman, Elizabeth and Carman, Neil J. *Cosmic Cradle: Spiritual Dimensions of Life before Birth*

Church, Dawson. *Communing with the Spirit of Your Unborn Child*

Hodson, Geoffrey. The Miracle of Birth - A Clairvoyant Study of a Human Embryo

Hallett, Elisabeth. *Soul Trek: Meeting Our Children on the Way to Birth*

Hallett, Elisabeth. *Stories of the Unborn Soul: The Mystery and Delight of Pre-Birth Communication*

Hinze, Sarah. *Coming from the Light: Spiritual Accounts of Life before Life*

Hinze, Sarah. *We Lived in Heaven: Spiritual Accounts of Souls Coming to Earth*

Kilby, Debra. *Rosa's Choice: A journey to the world of the spirit baby and how we can build a New Earth, together*

Nightingale, Christine. *Spirit Baby: What You Can Learn from Your Future Child*

Rogers Van Coops, Margaret. *Discovering your baby' spirit - A mother's guide*

Shaloe, Alison. *Baby Talk to Me: Spirit Baby Messages for the Journey to Motherhood*

Street, Kate. *What All Spirit Babies Want Their Mamas to Know: Otherworldly Wisdom to Support the Journey to Motherhood and the Journey to Awakening*

Walter, Makichen. *Spirit Babies: How to Communicate with the Child You're Meant to Have*

I learned about some of these books over 15 years ago, while some are newer. I even have met some of the authors in person, by email, and/or by Zoom on purpose. I have had Elizabeth Carman and Sarah Hinze as invited speakers for the 2017 Spirit Baby Summit - https://www.spiritbabysummit.com/. Some books were suggested by others as "must-reads." I use this list, plus more, for my Spirit Baby Academy students https://www.spiritbabyacademy.com.

I have not read all these books, but probably 90% of them. I have my favorites. Look over the list and see what resonates with your energy for in-depth support and immerse yourself in spirit baby insights.

What about all the fears that come up with spirit baby communication?

The biggest issue with spirit baby communication will be society and the culture that you are raised in that holds a negative belief about it. Your internal work is based on your external work and it will impact many choices, such as where you fit in, how you behave, and if you are allowed to be psychic. It is common in more developed societies that there tends to be a lack of self-awareness with an emphasis on new technologies and materialism that can lead to toxicities of mind, body, and spirit. That lack of self can bring a lot of doubt, health issues, and mental instabilities. This can cause you to feel you are not worth spirit baby communication. Remember, a very natural, instinctual bond of love between yourself and your baby is here. Don't get trapped by a fragmented and disempowering experience from your past childhood or current life experiences. It is only up to you to advocate for you and build your spirit baby communication relationship and move into deeper practices with it.

It is always really wise to remember that fear is normal. It is a biological response to something that causes physical, emotional, and mental reactions for your own safety. The body is set up with fear, and it can get out of control with chronic stress, leading to chronic fear caused by past or present reactions to life. Yet fear does not need to take up tons of space as you create spirit baby connections.

Many may feel they have a block or something is not moving, and it can feel impossible to move beyond how the mind interprets feeling blocked. However, the limitations are temporary. To believe requires doing something to change things and taking on healing in small and big ways to free the block and expand. You can do it and will do it because you have to do this. I never want to minimize or pretend that fear does not have its place, especially with trauma and difficulties in conception, pregnancy, and birth losses. Life gets intense and managing through the issues and opening with fear can offer productive and loving shifts as you create with your self-love and other loving practices of your own spirituality.

Spirit baby communication begins with the self and one's own ability to be open to it. It is supportive to recall and come back to viewing yourself as a healing part of nature and a whole and worthy of it. It begins with embodiment practices to nurture and ground yourself in spiritual practices like ritual and ceremony. Here you're going to keep learning how to soften into your layers so you can move forward. You can begin or continue to learn about your relationship to the earth, natural medicines to heal, trusting the biological intelligence of your body and mind, and showing up authentically through it all. Keep your motivation to listen, connect, and create with your own alignment with conceiving and birthing.

Am I doing it correctly?

I often get asked certain questions, especially about how to communicate with one's spirit baby. I can definitely say that insecurities will come up naturally, and my advice is to not get caught up in the insecurity; instead, be okay with it. Moving past this can take some reflection and changing energy practices related to how you want to set up your connection. It all depends on you.

I firstly would recommend meditation and a trusting awareness of your intuition. The medicine or antidote to insecurity is love and more love and doing it anyway with trust for being who you are. This helps create a successful experience that can bring about healing to empower and support your spirit baby journey with connection. Once you imperfectly allow self-trust, become more self-aware, and pay attention to your intuition, then you are ready to explore your colorful world of psychic space where your abilities to communicate move into another level.

What if my spirit baby is not around?

You are going to think about that. It can be deeply unhelpful to over-question with your mind. It can feel stressful to create a thinking pattern this way. You will do this from time to time and that is okay. The biggest part of spirit baby communication is trusting the conversations you are in creation with. Yes, you are going to keep reading about TRUST.

Sometimes spirit baby communication can feel one-sided, but trust that you are being heard because you truly are, and I have seen it over and over with parents in private sessions. Spirit babies make me laugh because they want so badly for their parents to know they are listening and hanging out with them, and they do this by sharing. For example, they may share silly things in the room, vacation trips taken, certain objects, celebrations, and more. They do this because only you would know.

Keep investigating what comes up and use meditation and other calming and opening tools and techniques to become skilled at it. Take a leap into faith with your spiritual connections. Your baby is more available than you may think, so it is time to feel and allow this. Remember, if you do not try, then you will never know or get it. It is never about perfection and always about learning and receiving.

How do I trust it is not my imagination?

What if I told you that you need your imagination to communicate with spirit babies... It can be very confusing, but yes your imagination is going to support how you communicate and what it means for you to trust the connection. I have a saying that your imagination, your dream space, and your psychic space all share a common connection with the mind, and they are only separated by a very translucent wall in-between them all. They move with each other. They need each other.

So stop telling yourself it is your imagination in a negative way as you could miss out! Remember to use your imagination and know that doubt, skepticism, and fear are going to be around. You get to decide how to trust and determine that all the other negative experiences will not be the leaders. You can and will do it. Your spirit baby needs you to do it.

Who am I and what is a Spirit Baby Medium?

I briefly spoke about this earlier in the book, and I want to continue with a bit more of the conversation here. One of the biggest questions I get asked is how I began this work as a Spirit Baby Medium and how do spirit babies share messages with me? It seems like one day I suddenly realized that there was this conversation happening with women in pregnancy and their babies with me. I actually did not think much about it until I began to share what I heard and sensed and experienced around these pregnant women. I thought it was just random thoughts as I was always very visual and had a colorful imagination. I was, in fact, using my psychic senses of clairvoyance and clairsentience to connect along with other abilities to sense, see, hear, and know through messages from the children in spirit and later to realize even in body after birth that children were telepathic and easily speaking through energy.

My own experience of becoming a mother has guided and gifted my ability to bring spirit baby communication to others around the world and to support experiences that bring new insights and more. In my pregnancies with my children, I had experienced pre-birth communication that was very different for each child with different communication styles. My oldest son, Rain, was highly visual with me and shared stories about himself. I could sit in meditation and he would show up instantly. In my visions, Rain had blue eyes and dark thick hair, almost like bangs. He would be born with blue eyes that turned green years later, and he had a lot of hair and was definitely not a bald baby. Rain was wildly active in pregnancy and still is today as an earthchild. My second son, named Forest, was very quiet and more timid and soft in my womb communication. He would communicate with me on his own terms. He was quiet, but very present and not available on demand like my first son. Forest would become a sensitive and keenly tuned-in observer as an earthchild. Their personalities matched my pregnancy communication in how they shared themselves.

Besides my experiences with my own children, other babies in spirit had all kinds of things to share with me and that would be from the kind of personality they would have, how they felt in their current growing body, and what their mother or father or sibling needed to hear. This was confirmed numerous times by mothers I met when working at a university and with friends of friends. It was met with accuracy and appreciation. I was not yet a Spirit Baby Medium, but seen as a common person who had psychic presence and knew things. Still, I did not fully step into that role until my own pregnancy and giving birth years later. I guess you can say that my early experiences were the beginning of my internship and practices. It was unconsciously led by intuition, which brought a deepening of my practice that would be an experiment to unwittingly become a Spirit Baby Medium.

The term "Spirit Baby Medium" came into creation through inspired thought to me one day, and it was not something anyone else ever used before. It was Walter Makichen, author of *Spirit Babies*, who revolutionized the now household phrase "spirit babies," in my personal opinion. He created a new consciousness when it came to conceiving and pregnancy, and birth loss with babies. His work has been celebrated globally through the popularity of his book *Spirit Babies: How to Communicate with the Child You're Meant to Have*.

As a Spirit Baby Medium, it became clear that what I did was not just serving spirit babies in the afterlife of death, but also serving spirit babies that want to be born upon Earth through conception into pregnancy. These spirit babies, I feel, are looking for a home to settle into, and they have a beating heart and a whole body to engage with and share on the Earth plane.

Being a Spirit Baby Medium is not just about having a psychic skill of future predictions or crystal-ball tarot readings. It is beyond immediate energy into possibilities that involve the ability to access different frequencies and the potentiality of human life through soul-to-soul communication and other unknown skills. The mediumistic tone to the work is bringing the spiritual world into daily life upon Earth.

How do I speak to spirit babies?

To understand how I speak to a spirit baby, you're first going to have to reexamine your mind and move away from the overthinking analytical parts of the left brain over to the intuitive visual, creative right brain. That right brain will be receptive to understanding what I am saying. It is the part where psychic presence or psychic space beyond the sensory system of the five senses (touch, taste, smell, hearing, and sight) can exist with awareness. It is in that space that I get to feel, hear, see, and know in a different way the in-between worlds of the before life and the afterlife. To give you a better understanding of the psychic space, it can be easy to understand what some would say I am: Telepathic,

Clairvoyant, Clairsentient, Clairaudient, and Claircognizant. I want to add that I also embody other unique traits not yet understood by thought and mind, and I will leave that for another conversation or perhaps another book someday.

How I perceive a spirit baby in conception, pregnancy, and miscarriage is very similar. It is later infancy loss that is different because these beings share a different frequency of presence and soul purpose. When I am ready to connect with babies being born or through loss, in most cases, I like to do this in a private session and not randomly "read" people off the streets or be psychically invasive in egotistical or playful ways. In a private session, I like to create an invitation with the parent or parents, which is typically the mother-to-be and/or father-to-be. This invitation aids how the session moves and helps it flow nicely. I ask spirit babies to come into this space to connect with me and their parent(s) in my energy and mind. I like to use a notebook while I listen to messages to read information through the field of energy. I am a very visual and deep feeler so information can move very quickly, and I do not want to miss it through sharing. So I write it down fast and draw pictures and color on my notebook. Before I share with parents, I have an already sketched out body image with space for notes. This is why I take the parent on a meditative-like exercise so I can listen in the relaxed space and "hear" what needs to come through and share it for energetic healing support.

When a spirit baby or babies are invited into the space, I like to look at it as an invitation because I have to invite that spirit and their full energy. This is whether it's one energy or two or three energies or more. It involves permission and holding a sacred opening with love that feels important for orientation and integrity.

With my spirit baby invitation, I sense the baby or babies and their presence as you would if someone walked into the room and stood next to you. The only difference is that there is not a body, but energy. I can sense the personality of the child or children, gender of girl or boy or no gender vibes. I telepathically speak to spirit baby or babies with questions and I listen and connect. I use my psychic senses and that language is translated in an easy way through words symbolically, metaphorically, and literally.

When I do perceive a child visually, I typically see a child between the ages of two years old to nine years old. I often am shown different things about spirit babies and their connections with the parent (or parents) and the bonding relationship. Spirit baby/babies share what I call a Soul Personality. A Soul Personality is something I made up to describe how a spirit baby shares messages as an already conscious being of experience and many parents feel, sense, and know that often before life. A Soul Personality is how a spirit baby communicates with us, and intuitive and psychic awareness picks up on the details of it. Babies will share their Soul Personality with every parent in the in-between worlds. It is who they will always be, whether they come into an Earth body or not.

I tend to see visually in my mind a child or children dressed in certain clothes, with hair and eye color coming through sometimes, and at times that is actually what they will look like. Other times I do feel it's what they want to share around their personality and the energy of who they are. For example: If I see a child dressed in playful, yet dirty clothes and no shoes, I know they are very casual and earthy. If I see glamor and fancy dress, it shows a more outgoing and creative energy. The clothes I see lead into deeper connections of being able to understand other fun traits: being sweet, humorous, healing, loving, wild, and/or quiet and peaceful. When I see this, it typically fits the personality of a child; many times it is confirmed that a parent has similar traits. Other times, it is confirmed after the baby is born and years later that the Soul Personality remains.

I have had spirit babies offer deeper qualities of themselves through how they want to bring their light into the Earth realms as peacekeeper activists, wise one teachers, creative builders, innovators, compassionate animal protectors, Earth guardians, timeline changers, and healers. I am sure more missions exist beyond my list.

What spirit babies share in messages varies greatly, and this is dependent on the needs and preparation of the awakened and healing parent's personal journey. As I am working with spirit babies, I am also working with the psychic energy of mother/parent. I am using my medical intuitive skills to tune into the body of individuals, starting from the top of the crown and working my way down through the heart, womb, and other energy centers. In that reading, I support the physiological, vibrational, and emotional tones of the past, present, and future. I feel like it's very important that I'm looking at everything that needs my attention and the messages that promote healing. I want the insights to impact the ways of healing and help prepare the way for a safe and trauma-free experience. My goal is to witness, see, and hold the experience for others, and provide ways to be with the spirit baby communication that keeps guiding the parent forward with confidence and love for what comes next.

I have had spirit babies share many interesting and mind-blowing things with my clients over the many years. I have spoken about it on my podcast, in person, and at other talk opportunities. I am always open and surprised by the uniqueness of women and men. I laugh about it because there are some things that seem really silly at times but are very meaningful for the mother or father. I have experienced babies sharing in pre-conception and conception (Trying to Conceive/TTC), and especially during pregnancy. They will share things that are in the home, like an odd-shaped vase, a sock, a decoration on the wall, etc. Other times, it will be foods they like or foods Mom eats that are specific, like popcorn, pizza, spaghetti, or sweets. I have had many messages of animals or insects, like butterflies, ladybugs, birds, foxes, dogs, and more. Even a unicorn and a mermaid have been shared! I have no control over how and what babies share and it can be fun. I have laughed many times in sessions.

Spirit babies are more than just a psychic conversation, but a true human baby waiting to or getting ready to come into creation within pregnancy and be born. I have never heard anything dark or negative or evil come up in any conversations with spirit babies, which is why I know that love and truth have no malice. That fear or other Earth manipulations and experiences do not exist in the before-life. Spirit baby energies tend to be beautiful, playful, loving, and joyful. That is what parents get to open up with and receive.

Spiritual Parenthood Begins with Spirit Baby Communication

Let yourself be immersed into spiritual parenthood. Allow what comes next for yourself and your baby or babies to come to you with ease and less effort. The intuitive psychic experiences are meant to change you, support you, guide you, and heal you. It will all keep coming together as you open with it and let the conscious heart of you lead your parenting journey. Remember that a new era of spirit baby communication is upon us, and it is time to get ready and let it unfold and come!

CHAPTER TWO

Messages from Spirit Baby

"Being a mother is one of the greatest experiences that you can have. It takes you to the length, breadth and depth of your being. You will never be the same!"

~ Margaret Rogers Van Coops, Ph.D., Discover Your Baby's Spirit: A Mother's Guide

The truth is our deepest learning comes from being born. Your birth sets you up with how you will feel and experience your bodily existence and how you will view the world around you. It is a new science to understanding the foundational time of birth and infancy, which are critical for how life develops after becoming an adult. I have been heart-gifted with much gratitude in providing sessions to others who were seeking answers and support and preparation towards parenthood. I have so many incredible, intense, and surprising stories to share. I have tuned into messages and energies of spirit baby communication for the parents and the spirit babies.

In this chapter, I will share stories pulled from the hundreds of sessions shared over a decade of spirit baby mediumship with parents and babies. In addition to the messages from babies, the sessions are about parent validation, evidence, and deeper healing. The stories are of conception, pregnancy, and birth loss. Some names of parents and babies have been changed out of privacy and others have given full permission to share their name and the child's name. I have supported women, men, couples, single moms by choice, and lesbian couples.

Natural conception into pregnancy after self-doubt (My story)

I am going to share about myself and my own pregnancy story of natural conception into pregnancy. I remember when I was opening up to conception and how I received my firstborn son after many months of active conception. My background story involves trauma like most of us. I feel like that can be saved for another book if it needs to be shared. For now, I am being very honest when I say that I was very fearful and unsure of my ability to conceive, and even if I was able to feel worthy of motherhood and open to receive unconditional (without any rules) genuine love.

Today we have many options with fertility testing and getting medical support, and ovulation kits, but when I was in conception that was not on my mind. It was something I never explored or understood. I decided to jump into trying to conceive without thinking and looking to see what conception would be and how I could become pregnant. I did not get any checkups and did not believe in invasive gynecological exams. I decided that I didn't want to do any interventions unless I needed it. I would tune into my body, pay attention, and see what would come next. It felt like that was what I was supposed to do. To listen to myself and listen to my body and baby. It was the best and wisest decision ever.

Instinctually, I called upon conception organically and energetically, because that is what I was connected to do. It felt natural and didn't require a lot of overthinking. I would give my womb love, and every night I would just take a few moments intuitively to see this beautiful crystalline energy filling my womb space by placing my hands on my lower belly. I envisioned a quartz crystal vibe. Eight months of active conception later, my son was conceived. Within a week, emotional energies and strong psychic communication would begin on a deeper level. I was pregnant and he was active in communication.

Natural conception into pregnancy, exploring the body, mind, and spirit (Colleen)

Colleen was a secret intuitive and bright hearted soul. She deeply struggled with conception and nobody knew why. She was told she had infertility. IVF was not in her heart. Nor did it feel like an option because she wanted a natural conception.

In one of our sessions, it was revealed that her issues were about her body structure and the energy shared in personal childhood moments that would create a subconscious story of not being able to conceive. This was the most profound session and it stayed with me for years.

I saw an image come up in the session of her as a toddler falling off the kitchen counter. I told her that she fell and her mother and father were in the room. The fall hurt her sacral lower pelvic area. It was not on purpose, but by accident. The toddler Colleen did not understand what happened. She heard her parents arguing. Her pelvic area within the muscles and tissues went into protection and holding. She could not process her experience beyond crying and tears.

Colleen's body and mind kept a nonverbal memory that would cause her body to hold conception back because it was not safe.

Colleen shares this about an earlier session...

"Thank you so much for an incredible session. I am very much in awe of your intuitive abilities and the subconscious mind! I called my dad after our session because I was very intrigued by your comment that you felt like my sacral injury occurred as a toddler. After our call ended, I kept thinking about that kitchen floor and I started to think that maybe I fell off the counter. I called my dad and told him I had an incredibly random question and subsequently asked him if I fell or was dropped as a child. He was a bit stunned by the question and said yes my mom placed me on the counter in the kitchen and I fell from the counter. I asked him if he was there and he said yes he was in another room. I asked him what happened next and he said he and my mom got into a huge argument. He said he 'went ballistic' on my mom for allowing that to happen. He said he can see how his reaction could have possibly left an imprint on me. I am so in awe right now – by your intuition and by my own subconscious mind."

After the many sessions we had together, Colleen decided to take some of the suggestions and move into natural remedies, different energy therapies, acupuncture, and work with her body's ability to release the energy from her past. In her experience over the years of infertility, she kept opening and healing for her natural conception to pregnancy. She made it happen, doing deeper childhood work that allowed her to heal through forgiveness, and so much more.

After the sessions, both Colleen, who shared with her husband her on-going experience both found a new inspired way towards preparing to become parents even though they were infertile for many years. Colleen would become pregnant with her daughter Maria and feel blessed by her sweet wonderous spirit.

Natural conception into pregnancy, exploring how energy healed infertility (Rebecca)

Rebecca was an empowered and vivacious mother-to-be, who was on a mission to conceive her children. She shared that she had been trying to conceive for about 10 years. Rebecca had two spirit babies, a son and a daughter, who would be in communication with us in each session.

Rebecca believed that the energy of healing was available for her. Every single day, she went deeper into the energetic frequency of how she could receive pregnancy, even after the struggle. In her few rounds of IVF, she had a loss and, with deep heartache, had to have a medical termination due to issues. She was open to trying IVF again, and this time her child was healthy and whole. The embryo development and it would be her son, who she felt was her first that she had to terminate. We were in communication with her son during conception into pregnancy, and he had a lot of beautiful, fun, joyful things to share. He supported his mother emotionally and prepared her with loving vibes into birth.

In the months after the birth of Rebecca's son, she was so thrilled and happy. Yet she could not get over a feeling of this other spirit baby who would always show up in our sessions, which was a girl spirit. Like most spirit babies, this little girl shared about emotional support, her own experience being in her world, and the healing energies that she could bring together with her mother.

Rebecca felt very fearful because she had been infertile for around a decade. She felt like IVF was not her option for this next pregnancy, but that she would have to work really hard to change the programming that said she needed intervention to conceive. That was what her body and mind believed. Not only did I tell her to open to the energy of natural conception, but so did her doctor even though Rebecca was in her mid-40s. There was no reason that she could not conceive based on her biology and based on her fertility. She was fertile, and so she opened up to it and was able to receive her daughter. Her daughter would be born, and now Rebecca has her two children on the earthside.

Having these pregnancies were such extraordinary experiences. Rebecca believed in herself and in the energy of her children, and she created the energy to heal and align with this. Her family feels complete.

Natural conception into pregnancy after delay (Nicki)

Nicki had a son who was eight years old, and she had been trying to conceive her second child for three years with her husband. She was diagnosed with unknown infertility. She had a private session with me and joined Cosmic Conception, a program at the time for spiritual conception.

Nicki was telepathic with her spirit baby being, who was sensed as a boy at times and a girl at other times. Nicki was determined to keep her energy open and the communication flowing. She would go deeper into her emotional connections with healing her past and not get caught up with too much stress of not being pregnant each month. She kept focused and allowed hope and faith to carry her forward. She did all the things you are supposed to do to conceive regarding mindset, bodywork, spirituality, and spirit baby communication.

After years of trying naturally, Nicki finally allowed herself to explore IVF. She read over everything involved and was ready to do it. One day she went for an exam to move into the next steps for IVF. Nicki's blood work came back that she was pregnant; she had ended up naturally conceiving. She was not only shocked but thrilled. Nicki was super excited to finally be pregnant after years of struggle and her daughter Bella would be born.

You never know what will come or how the journey will go. You just want to show up for it.

COUPLES

Couples conception into pregnancy (Luis and Jill)

Luis and Jill were a lovely and kind couple. They worked very hard to conceive their children. Jill was doing all the right things, like foods and exercise and working her best to de-stress her and her husband's lives. They still could not become pregnant.

Jill had many psychic visions, and she shared that she felt like she had a lot of psychic experiences as a child. In adulthood, Jill really connected with a sweet boy and a cheerful girl energy, and she felt that they were twins. So together we connected with her twins and received spirit baby messages from them. Each session together built Jill's frequency so she could heal and de-structure her belief systems and more.

Jill's dream had always been to become a mother because she grew up in a country where it felt important to have a family. She became deeply discouraged and even tried IVF with no success. She was traumatized by the experience with one clinic that pushed IVF, but after a new clinic she was open to trying it again. In our sessions, we created space in her energy that allowed Jill to be open to other possibilities.

Jill felt very strongly about her twins. Through IVF, she conceived twins, but they passed after a few weeks and didn't make it. Her heart was broken and fear set in, but she knew that becoming a mother to her children was not over. Jill decided to do something different and got her husband to be more involved with a new diet and exercise regimen. Soon after, the energy between them really shifted, and it allowed a new space in how she was in the partnership. They did later conceive a son first and next came a daughter, not as twins but as siblings. Jill knew these were her twins and her dreams of motherhood would become real. Jill and Jack were able to naturally conceive and birth their children after reproductive intervention and loss.

Intervention conception into pregnancy (Solace and Brad)

Solace and Brad were an amazing couple who had been trying for four years to conceive. They were doing it all right with vitamins, exercise, diet, and other holistic support. Solace could not understand why she was not pregnant. She felt her baby was so present. I connected her with a spirit baby boy in a session. He was kind, gentle, and talkative. The boy was very clear that he would be born through IVF. I hesitated to share this, but his message was very firm, clear, and strong. This spirit baby boy was confident in his conception.

Solace did not take this message well and was very saddened by it. I told her to explore why and her resistance. Her grief needed to be experienced until she decided to visit a fertility doctor. The doctor diagnosed her with tubal issues that were not repairable. Her medical issues made Solace a perfect candidate for IVF; after all her uterus was perfect and ready to receive conception.

Solace looked into doing natural IVF her first cycle, and the fertility clinic was in agreement to support her this way. Natural IVF uses a specific method with less intervention. She received her first transfer and after the two week wait, she was pregnant with her son. The spirit baby boy who shared his presence with us and how he would be born helped his mother be open to trying, even with fear and uncertainty.

Lesbian conception with spirit baby communication (Suzy and Jane)

Suzy and Jane were fiancées and they nervously sat before me. They needed to know who was going to be pregnant with their child or if their child was ready to come into their lives. I have learned to be honest and gentle with how I share messages. I saw a spirit baby with Suzy right away and he was strong and loud. He was hanging out with Suzy, but not Jane. Suzy was worried because she was older, and she wanted her fiancée Jane, who was younger, to carry their baby.

Suzy was surprised by the details I shared about her son and his connection with her. Suzy decided to share that she had an embryo that was from her egg and did IVF to transfer their embryo (boy) into Jane for pregnancy. For Suzy to experience this little boy in spirit standing next to her was confirming because the embryo from her egg and sperm donation ended up being a boy as we were communicating with in our session. They later conceived their son and Jane gave birth.

MISCARRIAGE/PREGNANCY

Healing intervention from conception into pregnancy (Nicole)

Nicole was 37 and did not find love until later in life. She was ready to bring her children into the world with her husband. She booked a session to get clarity about any blocks that were in the way of her becoming pregnant and then did multiple sessions for deeper support. Nicole was called to do IVF with retrievals that produced healthy embryos, but the transfers were not successful. She was very fearful not just in her conception, but anxious and a perfectionist.

Still, Nicole was beyond ready and wanted to deepen her relationship with her own psychic awareness, while accessing deeper emotional healing, and working with spirit baby communication. She had two frozen embryos and time felt important. Her two spirit baby beings shared themselves as a boy and a girl.

Her children spoke through telepathic (from one mind to another) communication, which is a common form of communication for the majority of parents, and also through other psychic senses. Nicole's spirit babies shared different colors that carried different messages each session for her personally and other healing insights to support Nicole.

A new transfer day came, and then Nicole had her two-week wait to confirm a pregnancy or no pregnancy. I remember, in our session at that time, Nicole had a spirit baby being that showed up right away in her energy, and it was a boy. Her spirit boy had crystal blue eyes and soft hair, and he had a very starseed like quality about him. Starseed is a unique soul with a mission that has roots within galactic realms that defy science. It is not uncommon for star-like or star-seed children to get their parents to come into sessions with someone like me who understands the star quality and connection. She got a positive pregnancy and gave birth to a boy.

The challenges of multiple miscarriages to pregnancy (Kate)

Kate was a mother already and she was a passionate and empathic soul. She had the intense experience of multiple miscarriages, which can easily fill a mother with chronic fear and distrust. She knew she was meant for another live child, but it was not happening. Kate had multiple sessions to go deeper. She worked hard and used her intuition, opening herself up to her spirit babies. She was able to feel, sense, and be loving as she navigated through the fear and allowed healing.

Kate shares this about a session...

> "Your guidance and connection to my future second child is what kept me going through my journey with recurrent miscarriage. I had four pregnancy losses, two of which were late-first-trimester losses. Both babies lost their heartbeats around 11 weeks; both were 'missed miscarriages.' Doctors found nothing medically 'wrong' with me. With my first 11-week loss, you had a little girl come through who showed you that the 'egg was no good.' A week later I received the D&C report that confirmed the gender of that baby had been female and that the embryo had a chromosomal abnormality.

"Then when I had my second 11-week loss directly after that, you had a little boy come through. You said that something in the chemistry of the body hadn't been right with that pregnancy, but that it probably wouldn't show up as anything abnormal on a report. When that D&C report came back, that baby had indeed been a boy and the embryo had appeared 'normal.' When you were connecting with that baby boy spirit though, you had said to me: 'He really wants me to tell you this, but I'm reluctant to say it, because you never know, but he wants me to tell you that he promises he won't do it again.'"

"This little boy was apparently referring to miscarriage – he promised that this was the last one as far as he was concerned. You also felt there was some significance surrounding timing in regards to my earthside son's birthday. Fast forward, and the next time I got pregnant, I was pregnant with a healthy baby boy (we named him Drew) who was born in December, the same month as his older brother. Drew kept his promise and didn't 'do it again.' It was simply amazing to experience this and so, so healing. To be determined if we ever bring that little girl earthside, who you've said is pretty intent on being born and is now 'behind her brothers,' but I'm just so grateful that we received Drew after all. Thank you for everything."

When Kate shared she was pregnant and her son Drew would be born, she kept staying connected to her spiritual heart and brought healing forward for herself and her earthchildren.

Miscarriage to pregnancy with spirit baby communication (Julie and Mark)

Julie and Mark were a loving couple that was ready to start their family. Julie was 42 and ready to become pregnant. She happily conceived her son without any problems, but at her 19-week scan he had no heartbeat. Julie was deeply pained by her loss and confused about her connection with spirit baby, especially after the loss. Julie shared how she felt that the loss of her son at first was unbearable and she didn't know what to do next. She then did some work on herself that brought a new sense of strength and ways to support others in the loss community. Like anyone with such a loss, Julie was fearful of her conception and next pregnancy. She had unmet grief to explore and feelings that were hard to hold. Yet Julie felt a deep love and openness with her spirit baby.

In our final session, she brought her husband, Mark. Julia and Mark waited for messages from their son, but it was a daughter who had much to share about herself and the connection with her mother and father. This sweet girl spirit was quiet in sessions until her father joined Julia. It felt deeply supportive for Mark to hear that his daughter was ready to play with him and surf. Spirit baby girl shared about surfing through messages, and Mark loved surfing and felt committed to a meditative spiritual practice after our session. This couple gained trust that the spirit baby boy would support his sister from pregnancy into birth. He did.

It is not uncommon for siblings to help each other in the spirit world. About four months after the last session, I received an email that Julia was pregnant and it was confirmed they were going to have a girl. She is now earthside, healthy, and thriving.

IVF - Creative Conception into Pregnancy (Kara)

Kara, age 40, had an older daughter and wanted another child. Kara was a grounded and loving mother. She did IVF and had an egg donor. Kara experienced a miscarriage with the IVF that was hurtful in her heart and confusing since this baby was very much welcomed. We worked together with sessions over months to connect her with a boy spirit and a girl spirit. She invited any gender to come into her family.

Kara's miscarriage baby in spirit shared in a session about a lake and swans. I thought to myself, *I am going to share this but it makes no sense to me.* That did not matter because it made sense to Kara. Kara shared that the day she miscarried, she found out after a lake visit that her baby was gone. She and her husband were visiting a lake, and very rare Trumpeter Swans swam by. The Trumpeter Swan is a very rare and special species to witness since they are very private and avoidant of people. This message from her spirit baby was confirmation that the spirit was very much connected to her. Later Kara did conceive her son and her family felt complete.

STILL BIRTH TO PREGNANCY

Still birth to pregnancy with spirit baby communication (Jade)

Jade came to a private session to find answers about her child, who had passed in utero at 37 weeks. Her son Bodhi was still born. Jade, just like any grieving mother, had her heart broken by the experience, and she was deeply in pain regarding how to live her life fully without her son.

Jade was concerned that her son felt pain when he died. I reminded Jade that it is normal to think about these things. In our session, Baby Bodhi shared himself as a sweet, kind, and gentle spirit. Afterward, he wanted his mother and father to know that he did not suffer. Bodhi shared that he had breathing problems and stomach issues.

He also shared about small trees, like bonsai. Jade told me that her husband owns a bonsai tree nursery. Bodhi, in communication, noted that he was always trying to get his parents' attention. He wanted her to know that he messes with the light outside the house's front door. Jade shared that they believed somebody was unscrewing the light bulb at their house. I told her that this was her son trying to communicate with her and get her attention.

This is why sign symbols and messages in the outside world are very important to be in tune with. Bodhi used energy to communicate in the physical world, and he would also share music and sounds in messages. This is something to stay alert to noticing. Jade later would go on to give birth to her daughter.

Still birth to pregnancy with the healing of communication (Garima)

Garima, a beautiful, nature-spirited being, suffered from a still birth of her son Ashwin or Ash, and after losing him, she had four other multiple miscarriages, one being ectopic. Her grief was very present, but over time we would create deeper healing. Ash was a powerful spirit and very open to communicating. He shared his light very brightly. He had much to share for his mother's heart healing.

I shared some hard details of how Ash's mother would birth him when he passed already. She confirmed the details. The messages were not always new information, but confirmation of the connection. In our sessions he was always present and ready to connect. He did share in a session that his mother would sing and she did.

I remember a session where he was very clear about bringing his sister forward. I knew a girl would be born, and I could sense her pregnancy was close, within a month or so. He would make sure his sister would get a supportive passage. It is not uncommon for siblings to support each other from before life to Earth. In some way, kind of like a guide or protector. Garima would become pregnant with her daughter, and sweet Aria would be born.

Garima shared her experience in a session...

> *"When we lost our son, we did not know finding Kelly was what we needed. Deep in our grief, I still remember the day she told me my son is telling me to let him go as I am blocking myself from receiving his sister, our now daughter.*

> *"Through deep work and sessions with Kelly, I was able to work on my grief, and also move forward to bring my two children earthside. She helped me balance and accept that grief and happiness can co-exist and helped me communicate with my spirit babies during pregnancies, which I felt privileged to be able to do. As I prepared to give birth, I felt that my one hand was helped spiritually by my son Ash that we lost and the other hand by Kelly who supported me from the days of grief to pre-*

conception, pregnancy, and then to bringing a living child home.

"I now have two earthside children. As I cherish them, my relationship built to the spirit baby world with the support of Kelly reminds me constantly that my sons Ash and Liam are still here, watching over us."

Garima had many losses. Her communication with her spirit children or children of light continues to grow and heal daily so that she can be present for her earthchildren. Her awareness and spiritual practices keep her heart solid and evolving. She keeps being in communication.

SINGLE MOTHER

Single mother conception with spirit baby communication (India and Karen)

(1) India came with desperation and a need for answers. Her sweet little girl came through IVF, and, in our sessions, her peaceful energy showed strong. This spirit baby showed me that she had slipped right out of her mother's womb. India was quiet, and I asked her if she could confirm that her girl was the embryo that slipped out. Yes, it was a girl embryo that was lost early on in a miscarriage. India was getting ready for another embryo transfer and she succeeded. She had a full term pregnancy and her baby girl was born.

(2) Karen, a single parent by choice, started at 50 and birthed at 51, going through IVF. She was highly intuitive and heart-authentic. She was committed to becoming a mother. Her first and second IVFs did not work. That left Karen regrouping and slowing down to make sure nothing was left

out to explore. Karen was committed and open to receiving her pregnancy. Karen's spirit baby boy was always in communication and shared many fun and playful messages. I remember seeing him one time on a train or subway in a sweet little button-down coat with his mom. She used transportation like that and I imagine this was a true moment as he made it earthside. Like he was showing me the future.

Karen shares...

"I often think of your vision of him on the train that you described. Exactly how our London metro-style trains are, with poles to hold on to. We call it 'the tube,' and it's mainly underground, but when you live farther out like we do, part of the journey is overground. Oliver has yet to go on a train. I have promised him he can go this summer."

Karen would become pregnant, and she gave birth to her boy. Her son, Oliver or Ollie, would be born healthy and with a great light of joy and pure love.

Conception, pregnancy, and birth loss healing are never a one-size-fits-all approach in the space of a session. There will always be a great mystery to the healing connections in the energetic and the unseen. What I understand in these private spaces is that I share not just psychic messages and conversations, but a frequency of love and ways for parents to continue to uphold their heart dreams and desires.

Connecting parents to their children has been an extraordinary way to support others. It's one thing that I do not take for granted. I am honored to be of service in this way. It is not just about my messages being shared, but the deep healing that gets experienced.

CHAPTER THREE

Intuition and Spirit Baby Communication

"And remember that for human beings the most potent growth promoter is not the fanciest school, the biggest toy, or the highest paying job. Long before cell biology and studies of children and orphanages, conscious parents and Seers like Rumi knew that for human babies and adults the best growth promoter is love."

~Bruce H. Lipton, PhD The Biology of Belief; Unleashing the Power of Consciousness, Matter & Miracles

My personal experience with intuition is that I never thought much about it growing up. But then at 15 years old I started to notice things, like outcomes and events that resulted in following my intuition and not following my intuition. I noticed that I had close calls but my intuition kept me safe, even if I did not fully understand it. I did not have to think a lot about it for it to work. I could understand how it brought more awareness to the way I saw the world around me. With the trust of my intuition, I experienced positive support in my everyday life. It was with me when I was in conscious listening; it was with me when I would take action when needed; it was with me when I was in the quiet of my mind; and it was with me as I would follow through with it. My intuition was my protector, and it moved within my own personal rhythm. As the years have gone by, I now know more about this natural part of what makes us all intuitive. I am intuitive and I trust it and nothing else and nothing more. I hope you do too, at least a majority of the time.

Intuition in conception, pregnancy, and birthing will be your best friend, and you're going to need it for your spirit baby communication relationship. Intuition is not magic or a New Age phenomenon. It is a real inner guidance that everyone has and honestly needs. Intuition is a natural instinct. As a guiding compass, it keeps one in safety and self-awareness. It protects us, saves us, and supports us. It supports us, even in ways we may not fully understand or comprehend at times. It is a natural innate messenger. This natural instinct does not need conjuring up because it is always there and it never judges and it never fears. (I will discuss fear and intuition more later in this chapter.) Intuition is with us from the start of life until the end. It is activated at birth. Some would consider intuition a science and biological response to our bodies and mind.

Albert Einstein, a physicist and the greatest influential scientist, shared that "the intuitive mind is a sacred gift and the rational mind is a faithful servant." In that intuition is our natural gift to knowledge. It brings attention to how society has brought worship to the pity of the mind that degrades the sacred or the Divine of who we truly are, I feel. Also, it feels important that the intellect does not take over the flow of our strong intuitive intelligence.

I often feel intuition can be hard to explain to others, but maybe a metaphor can help. When you walk outside your home, you feel the air and notice whether it is a breezy day or not. Intuition is like a gentle breeze that moves through the air, in that it is felt, somehow known, and experienced. Words can not describe the true state of being an intuitive person. Intuition is not just a self-awareness skill to work with; it requires listening, at times momentum, and other times solitude. It desires trust, the most from oneself. It never goes away, just gets hidden or denied or becomes dormant out of fear. Such fear may trick intuition into avoidance and resistance, or there may be a lack of an innate skill of awareness. Regardless, it is available.

Nikola Tesla, electrical engineer and inventor, did not only believe intelligence made him invent, but also his instincts. He said, "Instinct is something which transcends knowledge. We have, undoubtedly, certain fine fibers that enable us to perceive truths when logical deduction, or any other willful effort of the brain, is futile." I have included this to make you stop and reflect on how intuition has value beyond gold and money. It is the foundation and center of protection and guidance.

Intuition is activated more during pregnancy for many women and men too. It extends into motherhood, and a well-known term is "mother's intuition." Intuition will always be a guiding force in conception into pregnancy, and it is extremely supportive within miscarriage, still birth, and infancy death. I believe intuition is foundational. It begins with your baby self in the womb. You are born intuitive.

Intuition can be misinterpreted and the mind will challenge you with questioning being unintuitive or not intuitive enough, and that is not helpful. It is best to receive your intuition and acknowledge it with gratitude and confidence, to be humbled by nature and our instincts. Intuition is a building block towards self-awareness with spirit baby communication. It aids overall spiritual consciousness.

If intuition is being unintentionally ignored or not fully embraced, then obstacles and challenges will come up. That is a real problem which is not to be neglected. The challenges can be easily overcome with inner self-loving practices of connection and embodiment that are specific to safety, protection, and even inner child work. That means your intuition begins at birth. Yes, the moment you are born, your instincts are present. The next steps will be to keep operating within attunement as the child that gets to trust and explore through experience. The experience will be of the basic intuitive nature of life. The environment of others, typically parents and caretakers, has the biggest influence on how one serves oneself through being intuitive.

Intuition Is Crucial When It Comes to Spirit Baby Communication

You need intuition to work with spirit baby communication and your psychic awareness. That is because the spirit of a child is in communication through these specific senses of intuition. Your self-awareness in embracing your own intuition will help you be the best parent, and it can be the best gift to give your children. Remember that your center of intuitive guidance comes from:

- intuition of the mind,
- intuition of the heart,
- intuition of the gut,
- and intuition of the womb.

Your whole system is set up for intuition. That means it is time to use it and create a connection with your child.

You may be a beginner and new, or more advanced and experienced, when it comes to using your intuition with spirit baby communication. It does not matter. It doesn't have to be difficult, but requires trusting, listening, and taking action. Many need a self-awareness practice to build skill and presence. You can learn this and all it takes is time, practice, desire, and dedication to having your own experience in communication with the spirit of your child or children. It is okay to be excited by it, be doubtful, have fears, question it, and have other feelings and motivating curiosities about it.

Intuition Is a Love Instinct and You Got It

Your spirit baby is ready and open, and I am sure you are excited for your connection. Your obstacles will challenge you, and I want to teach you to soften into love over fear. Fear and intuition work against each other, and it is easy to misinterpret intuitive messages by stopping them and not listening. Be nice to yourself about it, and don't let fear create more fear. Just take a breath and come back to yourself.

When fear becomes intuition, then what happens is fear becomes the thing to trust. That means intuition will be pushed aside and fear will take over, hopefully not often. You will make choices out of fear and you have to be okay with that. My friend believes that fear can be an ally and guiding lesson towards personal actions. Those lessons you will learn, and you'll grow, and eventually you'll discover how to come back to you. So do not get upset or mistreat yourself. I'm not going to say it's going to be easy, but you can do it. The connection between intuition and fear will be unveiled through self-practices of listening and opening. I will say it again that fear is not intuition, and they are completely different. Fear and intuition do not speak the same language.

Remember, intuition is not something that needs to be obtained outside of you nor do you need training to become intuitive because it is happening right in this moment. So, for now, just breathe and trust. Trust that you are wired to be intuitive, become flexible about mistakes, and celebrate your wins. You are intuitive; accept it and be it.

Your spirit baby is not judging you for your mistakes and fears. You are a highly intuitive being, that already is a mother. If you feel you are not, then you need to have a heart-to-heart with yourself and have love connections with your spirit baby or babies. It is wise to know that your journey into parenthood begins before conception, but some get a crash course in conception or pregnancy. Your deeper self-inquiry will guide you into how to speak, connect, and receive messages from your child or children before life or in the afterlife. Your verifiable and authentic instinct center has got your back and communication is yours. It is here.

Your Psychic Awareness Habit Begins Today

Tuning into your intuition along with psychic awareness is your spirit baby communication, and, like intuition, you cannot have spirit baby communication without psychic awareness. I am going to show you more ways to connect and build your relationship and confidence with your child before life.

I want to add that my psychic awareness was discovered as a teenager. So I have been in a long-term relationship with my psychic self and development. As a teen, I observed the world around me very differently and how everything spoke with energy. I could feel it as my body buzzed physically and my head spun often. I began to know things and have visions and feelings about trees, animals, and people. I opened up to many metaphysical experiences and unexplainable occurrences. I just went with it, and I allowed myself, even at that age, to experience all these new and different things. I let them come through.

I was fortunate to not have to close it down. Instead, I allowed myself to talk about it with friends and other curious intuitives throughout the years. As the years went on, my psychic awareness became stronger and stronger, especially with self-assurance. My mind and body frequency began to shift more and more. That shifting took its own form into becoming who I am today. The unraveling of it all would take another entire book to share. For now, I will leave it and explore more psychic energies for your spirit baby connections and practices.

What Is Psychic Awareness?

Dictionaries define Psychic as: Someone that is sensitive to non-physical or supernatural forces. A medium, a channel, and a spiritualist. A psychic experience involves ESP (extra sensory perception) including telepathy, clairvoyance, psychokinesis, and or teleportation and more.

Psychic abilities are for everyone. That is right. Everyone is psychic in fact. I do not make psychic rules. They are not reserved for the special or gifted, and psychic experiences are all unique to the individual. Having psychic awareness is not a woo-woo or "far out there" ability to experience, but it can be regarded and perceived in wrong ways. Psychic awareness has been condemned by many religious and spiritual teachings for reasons such as: the occult stealing away self-preservation; or it is not acceptable or proper to believe in something that seems magical and mystical. As we know, that is not true, and a low vibration of thought comes from these ideas through insecurity and distrust of the self. Discernment is the guide, and I will leave it up to you to decide for yourself and what your heart shares with you.

Psychic abilities can be:

- visual,
- feeling sense,
- auditory,
- through other senses, such as smell and even taste.

Psychic awareness is often explained through paranormal and psychic phenomena. The "clairs" is a term used to explain these abilities of:

- Clairvoyance,
- Clairaudience,
- Clairsentience,
- Claircognizance,
- Clairalience,
- and Clairgustance.

I'll define each of these terms in the next section.

The Basic 6 is similar to your sensory system, but it is not the same. It lives in another part of the self and not the body or the brain. These parts can channel or sense in order to express it within words to communicate in a language of energy, signs, and symbols. You can even say that your physiological sensory system is connected to your energetic psychic system. Both your physical and psychic energetic systems are able to perceive the world internally and externally.

I am going to share a small part of psychic awareness to support how you can understand it from basic information. Through the past few decades, many new psychics have taken the spotlight in fame, fortune, and accuracy. Learn more through famous world-renowned psychics – mediums from history:

- Edgar Cayce,
- Richard Ireland,
- and James Van Praagh, to name a few.

Some Psychic Definitions

Below are some psychic definitions to help you get clarity and practice being in relation with your spirit baby communication practices. Psychic awareness is one of the many inner tools or skills that people are born with and open to as a child, but can close down into the adult years to hopefully re-emerge later when ready. Conception and pregnancy have a way of opening up what has been shut down.

Here are some defined meanings of the "clairs":

Clairvoyance means clear seeing. Clear seeing is being able to see in the past, present, or future within the Mind's Eye. The "Third Eye," it is often called. The clairvoyant experience often occurs in the hypnotic space of daydreaming and being in highly visual psychic experiences.

Clairaudience means clear hearing. Clear hearing can be with words, sounds, and/or music in the mind. Psychic sound can be perceived internally and through vibrations and tones. The clairaudience experience can be with awareness or without awareness.

Clairsentience means clear feeling. Clear feeling is being able to feel emotions, physical sensations from others, and other energy kinesthetic experiences. Psychic feelers are often known as Empaths and Sensitives. Psychic feelers can experience both positive and negative energies.

Claircognizance means clear knowing. Clear knowing is being able to perceive and experience information that just shows up out of nowhere. That can sometimes be a premonition. This can often be a very challenging ability because you have no feeling or vision or sense; it's just a deep knowing.

Clairalience means clear smelling and Clairgustance means clear tasting. The senses of clear smell and clear tasting are exactly what you think they are. It is being able to psychically taste and psychically smell things that are not in the physical environment around you. This ability can happen when you are interacting with other people and from the other side or afterlife.

Examples of smells are:

- perfume,
- smoke,
- or flowers.

These things are not in the physical space, instead psychically shared by loved ones or spirit babies or others.

Examples of psychic taste include:

- tasting in your mouth.
- strong flavors of bitter or sour or sweet

Again, this is without having any food in your physical body or space.

All the "clair" or clear senses are highly important. I understand that most people may resonate with some psychic abilities over others or you may question all of them. You are able to develop connection with your psychic awareness in many different ways through practices of embodiment and practices of meditation and other psychic exercises. If you want to explore more, look into **clairvoyance theory, psychic recognition, psychic cognition, psychometry, and telekinesis.**

Your Baby Is Ready to Communicate with You

Spirit baby is ready to communicate. When you feel disconnected to your psychic side, it is because you have not felt safe enough to explore. In childhood, many are psychically free and not held by any rules, but often later get shut down and hopefully come back to it as an adult. Sometimes life-changing traumas, a damaging lack of self-esteem, massive fears, and other major insecurities shut it down, but hopefully it can be temporary. I do not want to minimize your fears that can create hard blocks or inhibit your ability to access that safe and trusting psychic loving space. Owning and becoming a psychic exploring will guide you into how you get to build your psychic lifestyle. Remember to not be limited, fearful, or tempted to run from yourself. Everyone has spiritual and psychic abilities, remember that. So do you!

Psychic awareness is your everything within your spiritual communication with your spirit baby or babies. To begin your psychic awareness training is to remember who you truly are and what this energy of seeing, feeling, knowing, and sensing are about. I have taught for many years how to access one's best way to open up and remember how to use your psychic communication with intuitive awareness. I have the ability of all the "clairs," and I have experienced all at one time or another, even the smell and taste, especially in messages for other people. I use my more prominent ones that I feel secure in – Clairvoyance, Clairsentience, and Claircognizance – to support baby spirit and mother and/or father and to share energy from medical intuition.

Getting ready to master your psychic awareness begins now with exploring your psychic communication ability. What kind of communicator are you? What clair spoke to you the most? How do you use that sense to communicate and feel confident? Remember to be curious and do not get caught up by overthinking or over-questioning or feeling too much doubt. Be open and keep relaxing into your psychic spaces and receive messages of support and love. You can do it!

Psychic Spirit Baby Communication

- Your psychic intelligence is within you.
- Practice self-awareness.
- Explore books, classes, podcasts, and groups.
- Practice with other people and share in psychic readings.
- Sit in meditation with your body, mind, and spirit.
- Create with it; sing, chant, and/or dance with it.

You are the master of your intuitive psychic space. I will guide you into spirit baby communication with loving and pure tips and exercises to create a practice for conception into pregnancy, and healing birth loss if this is your experience. Each specific chapter forward that pertains to your experience is meant to promote your personal healing practice into communication, connection, and heart awakening. Go into it with gentleness and openness because what influences you the most within your ability to communicate with spirit babies is the past, the present, and the future. Meaning, your own birth from embryo into life, how you grew up and were raised, your societal and cultural beliefs, the life experiences you create, and more. I know and believe that you can create a relationship with your children before life and afterlife with your baby.

CHAPTER FOUR

The Art of Spirit Baby Communication, Part 1 & An Introduction to the New Children of the Earth

"Spirit Babies can talk and communicate because they have developed these skills over many lifetimes. Rather than an infant, the spirit baby is more like a seasoned traveler who has learned to speak many languages and adapt to many situations."

~**Walter Makichen, Spirit Babies: How to Communicate with the Child You're Mean to Have**

We all have to begin somewhere. You don't have to be the best spirit baby communicator, and you don't have to be the most connected. But you definitely do have to release your mental energy, your overthinker, and the controlling part of yourself in order to have an experience of speaking and receiving messages with spirit baby energies. I believe that we can all own self-mastery with spirit baby communication. After all, it is your own internal remembrance into the multidimensional that allows you to have these rich and present experiences of connection and love.

Do not become confused by or feel insecure about your new exploration with spirit baby communication. Go into it with openness and understand that you are ready and it is not unattainable. Remember that you are showing up every day to real and present experiences with spirit baby communication. You get to question, lead, hesitate, solve, let go, and welcome your experience. I believe being unsure of your experience and being fearful is just a shift into being empowered and motivated towards your heart of spirit baby.

Who are the New Children of the Earth?

Before exploring more about spirit baby communication, I want to share about the New Children of the Earth. These children are not like children of the past. They are meant to change our world through their own spirit coming into creation and being a part of this time and the future.

Here's a helpful definition…

A New Earth Child is:

- on a personal mission with their own agenda,
- karma-free (yes, that is right) and an embodiment of pure LOVE,
- a frequency that vibrates purity,
- an Empath in a positive and sensitive trauma-free way,
- an electromagnetic disruptor to change matter,
- deep-minded and with a heart capacity that is limitless,
- a natural intuitive and psychic in a matter-of-fact way,

- capable of receiving interdimensional truths and light language effortlessly, and
- born with remembrance and wisdom to share.

You are ready to become a parent and be called Mother or Father if you have not claimed that name yet. Your new earth child or children are getting your attention already. I trust that to be true for you because you have been called to explore spirit baby communication. You may have already been pulled by feelings and random mental images, daydreams, sweet meditative spaces, and/or quiet telepathic or inspired thoughts. You may have had your sleep space visited with nighttime dreams of messages and signs. Maybe you cannot shake off that feeling or how your mind keeps thinking about babies. It is because your fantasizing may be more than just that. This is your New Earth Child reaching out to you.

Your Spirit Baby Hears Your Heart Call

Spirit baby communication begins with desire. Such communication can be medicine for your heart and soul. Tell yourself, "I trust this mystery of life before life" and "I am open, I am ready, and I am available to love and to allow." You are ready to welcome new connections.

Parent(s)-to-be have many different spiritual skills to gain and use, while opening to new undiscovered parts of the self through pre-parenthood healing. You are being asked to trust and drop inward to the Spark of life coming from some Divine place in some other part of the Universe or through your faith and trust in the ultimate creation of a loving Source. If you are on the search for how to connect with your baby or if you have the ability to learn, then you are on the right path.

Spirit babies are more than just a baby spirit – rather a whole beautiful being. Baby spirit comes with a mysterious mission that you are not supposed to know or have all the details or answers about. That way, it keeps you aligned with living together with the greatest adventure of spiritual learning and life expansion.

Spirit baby communication can begin right now or it can be something you started years ago within pre-conception, active conception, pregnancy, and/or after-birth loss. Everyone connects with spirit baby or babies in different ways. For example, I use my different "clair" abilities as I shared in the earlier chapter. So I can translate my sensing self by using images, symbols, feelings, and sharing those energetic stories and messages. My practice has been finely tuned and that relationship is growing with greater accuracy and psychic intelligence. In your case, embodiment, meditation, and relaxation are going to support your connection with trust and spirit baby communication skill-building.

You may not always feel good about your spirit baby communication relationship. It is easy to feel lost or distracted by insecurity, an overthinking mind, or stress. This is why meditation works well as a platform toward self-awareness into self-discovery and embodiment connections. I encourage you to create your own practice that trusts intuition, uses awareness, and is open with spirit baby and how you communicate. It is okay to feel challenged by fear and stress, just come back to it. Get your body and mind into easeful and peaceful states for connection. Spirit baby communication is your heart practice and spirit baby is waiting for you to connect.

What is your best path to spirit baby communication?

The best way to communicate begins with listening, and not just listening with the mind or thoughts, but listening with your whole body. You are a full-sensory person, and you need to activate and connect with your whole system that senses and expands into information and messages with you and your spirit baby.

You are ready to build your communication with your spirit baby or your baby being or your child of light. First, you will need to get clear on how you connect and communicate because it will guide you and support your steps upon your spiritual journey.

Remember in Chapter 3, you learned that your psychic and spiritual sense will work best with confidence and lets add joy to elevate your energy with communication with spirit baby. You can review the previous chapter that goes into the psychic self and apply it to yourself, and then use your extrasensory perception to learn and refine it. Here is your reminder of the "clairs": (not limited to) Clairvoyance (clear seeing/inner vision), Claircognizance (knowing), Clairaudience (auditory sounds), and Clairsentience (empathy/sensing feelings). You can use all or some of these abilities to connect with spirit baby, and you get to experiment and see where nature takes you.

What ways do you connect or feel you will connect with spirit baby? What new ways can you learn to incorporate to develop a stronger bond? You will be learning even more ways in the pages ahead.

Once you tune into your spiritual sensitivities, then you can master your way of knowing your baby or babies. Remember, everyone will communicate differently and not one person is meant to connect the same. I feel this is highly important to remember and to understand, because you are a unique being that listens to your intuitive psychic energies and uses them daily.

What messages does your baby want to share with you?

It is a very special and deeply connecting experience that your spirit baby or babies wants/want to communicate with you, whether you are in pre-conception, pregnancy, or healing after loss. The messages a baby shares can be quite simple or much deeper. Your baby is connecting with you on the deepest level of love. It can be hard to give words to the love frequency that is in your own heart and that you are opening and receiving with. You are healing together, and you are awakening together, and you are building creative forces together.

You may receive messages as:

- telepathic visual images or words, that lead you into noticing certain animals or insects getting your attention
- numbers that keep showing up that invoke feelings
- colors that you see outside around you or within your mind's eye, and other hypnotic daydreaming experiences
- nighttime dreaming
- pop-in-your-head messages of words and/or phrases
- more symbols and signs

Understand, it will vary as you grow within your communication.

You're meant to receive your insights with openness and curiosity, even if you are not sure at times or feel untrusting or skeptical. Doubt and fear will be in this journey of spirit baby communication. It is what you do with the fear and/or doubt that makes you open or closed down to your heart's path of parenthood. Remember that insecurity is temporary, and your love with your baby is infinite. I believe in you and you are going to do it.

What are some of the messages shared that parents have experienced with spirit baby communication?

- Mommy, I'm here.
- I'm ready to come.
- We are healing together.
- I am helping Daddy heal his heart.
- I send birds to you.
- I send butterflies.
- I send rainbows.
- I make things in the room move.
- I'm right here.

I have had many sweet statements or messages from spirit babies...

Here are some shares:

Conception communication with spirit baby: Mom, "I am playing with bubbles and the floor is covered in bubbles." What does this mean? Mom confirms that the carpets are being cleaned right now as we speak. Spirit baby is confirming that "I am here."

Conception communication with spirit baby: Mom "has these strange drinking glasses or vases." What does this mean? Mom confirms that last night they found strange drinking glasses in the back of the cabinet and laughed about it. Spirit baby is confirming that "I am here."

Conception communication with spirit baby: Mom, "check your thyroid." What does this mean? Mom's previous testing showed the thyroid was okay, but she decided to test again. The test confirms Mom's thyroid levels are off. Spirit baby is confirming that "we are connected and supporting each other."

Conception communication with spirit baby: Mom "has no eggs." What does this mean? Mom confirms, "I have no eggs in my ovaries and do not ovulate." Spirit baby is confirming that "We are connected and supporting each other."

Conception communication with spirit baby: Mom, "Dad's sperm needs help." What does that mean? The sperm is irregular or low mobility. Spirit baby is confirming support for Mom and Dad.

Pregnancy communication with spirit baby: Mom, "I like it when you eat popcorn and chocolate." What does this mean? Baby is confirming that "I am here."

Pregnancy communication with baby: "Dad likes Superman." What does this mean? Mom shared that Dad has a Superman collection in the home. Baby is confirming that "I am here."

Pregnancy communication with baby: Mom, "please dance." What does this mean? Mom, I am a dancer. Baby is confirming that your communication is dance and also "I am here."

Pregnancy communication with baby: Mom, "Daddy is a funny guy with digestion issues." What does that mean? Baby is confirming that "I am here and I can support you both."

Birth loss communication with child of light: Mom, "keep a look out for snails." What does this mean? Mom confirms a cemetery visit that week with snails all over the headstone of the baby boy. Spirit baby is confirming that "I am here."

Birth loss communication with child of light: Mom, "my sibling is coming." What does this mean? The sibling is sending a sister or brother. Spirit baby is confirming that "I am here."

Confirmation is what spirit baby needs from you to acknowledge that they are here with you, even if you are unsure or question the communication. Baby wants you to bond and build your natural love connections. Messages do not need to always be some profound spiritual truth, and they can easily be simple and in the moment. Again, it's about receiving, knowing, and trusting.

Am I making it all up?

The biggest question I hear all the time is "Am I making it all up?" What if my wish or dream is making me believe I am in communication with spirit baby? We live currently in a world that is intellectually driven and that means logic gets the strongest say, but not everything needs logic to be real and true.

It is easy to believe that somehow you made it all up, but what if you are wrong with that thought? Then you miss a true opportunity for communication. You want to be mindful not to judge yourself with feelings of insecurity or an obsession of resistance. Otherwise, you accidentally allow yourself to ignore or pretend it was just your imagination and miss out. You do not want to miss out because you cannot surrender your held belief and allow yourself to open just enough to experience a profound connection of communication and messages to support your path from your child or children.

Overall, I highly encourage the use of your imagination. Your imagination is everything. What do you think clairvoyance is? It is imagery in messages. I have learned that imagination shares space with real life, dreams, psychic visual experiences, and mental thoughts. Meaning, that a fine line exists between each, with invisible subtle boundaries. Your own discernment is wired inside you, and that is how you know the difference. At other times, you may not know and nothing is wrong with that also. You have choices that are available with your imagination as a healthy part of spirit baby communication practices.

You have to show up for yourself. It is okay to question your connection and what you see and sense. Remind yourself that the use of imagination and psychic awareness can feel illusionary, but it is not. Psychic experiences can be hard at times to decipher, but also accurate, evidential, and validating. It may take work to trust and move deeper into that as your own truth.

The before life of spirit baby, we must remember, is aligned with a deeper mystery. Even philosophers, teachers of science, and mystics have tried for centuries to understand the meaning of life and the people in it. The language will keep changing, and getting a better idea and understanding will continue to inspire us and help us learn more. Spirit baby communication experiences require beyond-the-ears listening and a level of trust that you get to build over your life with new experiences, self-kindness. and self-love.

CHAPTER FIVE

The Art of Spirit Baby Communication, Part 2 (More Tools)

"The realm of unborn children is invisible to "normal" human senses. Like a scientist piercing subatomic particles with an accelerator, women with an expanded awareness transcend ordinary perception and see into a subtler dimension. Such mothers feel blessed to begin motherhood by welcoming and connecting to their child before birth."

~ Elizabeth M. Carman and Neil J. Carman Cosmic Cradle - Spiritual Dimensions of Life Before Birth

Tips for Spirit Baby Communication - Next Level Intuition

You've now become a master of your intuitive psychic space, and you're getting a deeper understanding of what spirit baby communication is. The next step is to further explore your communication style. Your communication style involves your psychic self and the different ways you receive messages. It is exciting that you and your baby and/or babies are in communication. You will be using your psychic awareness, which includes other practical exercises and activities, to construct and engage a new experience.

I have mastered my style of how I psychically connect and how messages are received by myself to share from spirit babies. I have received many messages from spirit babies from all over the world for so many parents, and the babies will create communication not just through meditation in a visual-sensing space only. There is also music, singing, art, dance and movement, writing and journaling, gardening, walking, hiking, bodywork, and even knitting and cooking. Yes, I have had these things shared from babies in conception and in pregnancy. I was surprised on more than one occasion when other babies said Mom should knit so they could connect. Luckily, these particular moms did happen to be knitters, and that was confirmed after I mentioned this message from spirit baby. So anything goes in the spirit baby world and don't doubt it. Just continue to be open to what messages your baby or babies want to tell you.

So what do you need to begin communication?

Meditation! It's the number one thing you are going to read and hear about when creating a spirit-baby communication connection. Meditation is the best place to start and begin, but maybe you're asking what kind of meditation? How do you do a spirit baby meditation? Am I doing it right?

You can do any kind of meditation. It can be a meditation that uses visualization, guided imagery, Transcendental Meditation, walking meditation, Qigong, Buddhist meditation, yoga, mindfulness meditation, Tai Chi, and more. When you're in a space of meditation and feeling calm and open, then you can create your spirit baby communication practice.

Many prefer to experience spirit-baby guided visual and sensing meditations, which I teach with others in private sessions and through workshops and programs. I know it can be super supportive to have a specific spirit-baby guided meditation and extremely helpful to experience and practice with. I will have free meditations available for you to access at the end of certain chapters throughout the book with an easy link to follow.

The meditations will be useful for conception, pregnancy, and birth loss healing. I am going to go deeper into other ways of communication that you may find supportive and something you may have experienced yourself already.

Your spirit baby communication practice can include different practices to develop and gain deeper trust. That way, you can secure your approach towards meeting and knowing your baby's personality and sharing your love.

Ways to Use Communication - Creating Practices with Psychic Methods

COLOR COMMUNICATION

What is color communication?

Color communication is receiving messages of colors, whether it is physically outside in the external world or more internal in meditation. When you experience color as communication, it can come at different times in different ways. It is best not to over-interpret or try to figure out too much by reading books on color and signs because everyone is different. Let the colors guide you. You can receive colors spontaneously through daily intuitive experiences and/or create a color together with your spirit baby.

Color Method/Exercise- A Sample to Practice With

- Buy colored paper or make your own with paint, crayons, or markers.
- Shuffle through cards with your intention of spirit baby guiding you.
- Ask your baby to pick a color or colors. Whatever card you pick is correct.
- Use those cards to connect and bring that color into your body and mind.
- Have a conversation with your spirit baby.
- Try not to overthink or analyze.
- Remember each color has a meaning for you. Try not to look up the meaning of colors. Go with your gut!

Using colors has supported many parents with this kind of communication. If it is new, explore it and see how it goes. Remember that it's more than just a color. It's a message to you and with you. There are so many shades of colors, from light to dark. Keep open to listening to what is shared and how you receive it.

Conception communication with spirit baby: Mom, "I am a rainbow of light." What does this mean? Mom, I just saw double rainbows and see them everywhere now. Spirit baby is confirming that "I am here."

Pregnancy communication with baby: Mom, "I always see green." What does it mean? Mom feels it is a message for her heart *chakra that means love and connection. Baby is bonding and communicating to build a relationship.*

ANIMAL/ INSECTS COMMUNICATION

What is animal/insect communication?

Animal or insect communication is receiving messages from the living kingdom of creatures such as butterflies, hummingbirds, foxes, bunnies, frogs, horses, dolphins, and more. Animal messages or "animal medicine," as I like to call it, comes in different healing ways. It could be in a daydream, through meditation as a vision, during your daily activities of life, or even in nighttime dreams. Animals and or insects are not just the real life you see out your window. They can also come through pictures, someone else mentioning it, and even through other friends and family sharing a story about it. Spirit baby communication with animals can be very guiding and supportive. Your obstacle will be your mind, and it is very easy to overthink the connection. But when you can feel into the message, it is meant to be.

Animal Communication Methods/Exercises

- Go on a walk, talk to your spirit baby, and ask for an animal message.

- You can use cards/decks with animals on them from a kid's deck or an oracle deck. Ask what animal message your spirit baby wants to share with you.

- Spirit Baby Oracle deck has an animal communication card and other creative messages that can support communication guidance.

- Be open when you ask because messages can come up through pictures, conversations, dreams, or other signs from friends and family.

Remember, animal communication can come to you through a conversation with somebody, seeing an animal outside, images that may be sent to you, and/or other spiritual ways. Animal communication also can include pets that you have connected with in this world and other worlds, and babies that are in communication with those fur babies. The animals/insects that come to you through communication are not limited to what I share here, which is what I have witnessed. I have seen a snail, many butterflies, ladybugs, lizards, owls, a wolf, and all kinds of birds.

Birth loss communication with a child of light: Mom, "I send you butterflies." What does this mean? Mom, I see so many butterflies, from friends, in pictures, one time in Winter, and more. Spirit baby is confirming that "I am with you."

Pregnancy communication with baby: Mom, "I send you hummingbirds." What does this mean? Mom keeps seeing hummingbirds and it makes her feel warm and connected to her baby. Baby is confirming that animal communication is saying "I am okay."

NUMBERS & SYMBOLS COMMUNICATION

What is numbers or symbols communication?

Numbers or symbols communication is receiving messages that can be mathematical or symbolic. Number communication involves repetitive numbers that are seen over and over, whether it's through clocks, different license plates, in dream space, waking up to certain numbers, hearing alarms go off with certain numbers, having mail come with certain numbers – just to name a few examples. Symbols can be shapes and geometric patterns. You're seeing those numbers and or symbols are not just random; so be open to it.

Numbers & Symbols Communication Methods/Exercises

- Ask spirit baby to send you a number or symbol, whether in meditation or outside in your daily life routines. Be open to how it arrives.

- In meditation or when daydreaming, you can ask for a number or symbol to come into your mind.

- For nighttime dreaming, you can ask before bed for a number or symbol to come to guide you.

Remember that your communication with numbers is about receiving and allowing whatever that number means to you to come through. It is quite easy to look at numbers through numerology or books, but I encourage in spirit baby communication to tune into a number that is connected to you. You can reach out and ask spirit baby for a number to help guide you.

Symbols and patterns can be guiding communication messages, and they require your ability to be open and receive without overthinking. Just allow it to come. Symbols, for example, could be shapes like stars, circles, squares, ovals, other geometric patterns and lines, and more.

Conception communication with spirit baby: Mom, "I send you numbers." What does this mean? Mom, I see the same number on license plates, cell phones, and even receipts. Spirit baby is confirming that "I am here."

Conception communication with spirit baby: Mom, "I send you shapes." What does this mean? Mom, I triangles and star shapes all the time and sometimes spirals. Spirit baby is confirming that "I am here."

JOURNALING & WRITING COMMUNICATION

What is journaling or writing communication?

Writing communication is receiving messages through the writing of:

- letters,
- words,
- phrases in forms of automatic writing,
- journaling,
- stories,
- and/or poetry.

Psychic writing communication is often called "channel writing" or "automatic writing." This form of communication can be done very simply with pen and paper or with hands on a keyboard.

Writing communication begins with opening the energy to the space and knowing and trusting that spirit baby is in telepathic communication with you. Allow the words to move through your mind onto the paper and trust your connection. Know that baby being is guiding you towards deeper levels of connection. In a channeled writing space, many like to begin with prayers or an intention and then just begin to write. Let the words guide you. Then write together.

Journaling Communication Methods/Exercises

- Start with a calming breath and get your journal or writing pad out.

- Use pens or markers to write or use a notepad, scratch pad, or electronic device.

- Beginning with creating a statement:
    - "Dear Spirit Baby.... I am here, I am ready, and I am open." Add some of your words to this to get the energy of writing going. It may be easier to write while sharing your feelings about your spirit baby.
    - Let the words come and keep writing and writing.

- Eventually, you can ask your spirit baby for messages and have a back-and-forth conversation.

Remember that writing communication will come in an inner voice of your own, but it will have a different energetic quality that is not your usual. Try not to get lost in overthinking and think fluidity and ease. You can teach yourself to be in writing communication and allow the practice to unfold and guide you.

Pregnancy communication with baby: Mom, "I am writing with you." What does this mean? Mom, I journal and write letters with you. Spirit baby is confirming that "I am in communication with you."

Conception communication with spirit baby: Mom, "Journaling with spirit baby feels strong." What does this mean? Mom, I journal with spirit baby all the time. Spirit baby is confirming that "I am here."

MOVEMENT & DANCE COMMUNICATION

What is movement and dance communication?

Movement and dance communication can be a missed opportunity if not listening. In many cultures, movement and dance tell a story, and a spiritual experience can be birthed from it. Movement and dance communication is receiving messages through the movement of the body, whether it's yoga, a dance practice, or other spontaneous dance.

It is not common to think that spirit baby communication can be more active in the body, but, of course, it can. Your spirit baby can influence you to use movement and free-flowing dance to create communication through a new or old practice. It is a feeling or thought that comes into your mind to be creative in dance and you follow it or not. If spirit baby communication through dance is new to you, here's how you would begin to create a practice.

Movement Communication Method/Exercise

1. Begin by creating a prayer/intention. Also, decide if that includes music or silence.

2. Find a space that allows movement and use music or no music.

3. Ask your spirit baby to guide your energy into movement.

4. Step into the movement and see what your body does with your spirit baby serenading or otherwise guiding you.

5. Move together and experience what wants to come forward and receive creative force and co-creative energy together.

Using dance in spirit baby communication can be a deeply healing and energizing experience. Movement or dance with spirit baby communication can offer ways to heal that deepen the mind and body. The energy of the body has a story.

Conception communication with spirit baby: Mom, "I communicate through dance." What does this mean? Mom, I am a dancer and dance. Spirit baby is confirming that "I am here."

MUSIC & SOUNDS COMMUNICATION

What is spirit baby communication with music and sounds?

Music and sound communication begins with receiving messages that are connected to frequency vibrations and tones. Music communication can also use lyrics and songs and/or musical instruments, such as drums, violin, or piano. In addition, spirit baby communication through music can involve being in meditative spaces and letting it guide you into communication.

Something powerful happens with music communication because the body relaxes and opens. Sometimes the messages in the music offer meditative insights that can come forward not just through the lyrics, but also through your own voice of song and poetry. You do not need to be a professional musician to have spirit baby communication with music and sounds, but you can if you are.

If you want to include music in spirit baby communication into your practice, try the following:

Music Communication Methods/Exercises

- You can speak to your spirit baby in your mind or outside with your voice. Say: "I am here. I am connected to you, and I am listening." Then turn on the radio or music app from your phone and see what spirit baby picks for you.

- You can find a song that you feel is for you and your spirit baby.

- Sit in your heart space and let that connect you both with humming or your own singing.

- Adding dance communication with spirit baby music communication together is another possibility.

Remember to drop into your body and let the music guide you. You're letting your heart send out that spirit communication energy so that you can listen and or be still or use movement. The communication is back and forth in a trusting practice and keeps evolving to give guidance.

Conception communication with spirit baby: Mom, "I am playing the guitar." What does this mean? Mom confirms that she and her husband love music, and he plays the guitar. Spirit baby is confirming that "I am here."

Pregnancy communication with baby: Mom, "I am playing the piano." What does this mean? Mom confirms that she uses music to relax and plays music. Spirit baby is confirming that "I am here."

ART COMMUNICATION

What is spirit baby communication with art?

Art communication begins with receiving messages through art. I call it "Psychic Artistry." You are using your own psychic connection to make art using your mind, your eyes, your breath, and more. Spirit baby communication loves to connect with creativity and art. This can include art projects, whether it's through sculpting, drawing, coloring, or any other medium of art that provides a deep connection with your own creative force with baby communication. Psychic Artistry has a limitless potential when it comes to connection and communication.

To create a psychic artistry experience with spirit baby communication, try something that I have taught before in a program called the Spirit Baby Immersion.

Art Communication Method/Exercise

1. Get a large blank piece of paper and gather markers, pens, pencils, paint, and/or crayons.

2. Set an intention of love and drop into your heart.

3. Ask your spirit baby to create with you and let go into what comes upon the paper.

BONUS ITEM: I like to print out images and pictures of infants that are line-drawn so I can then add colors to it or words or phrases. You can add sparkles, stickers, decals, and more.

Remember, no perfection is necessary in this art, and you do not need to be a professional artist. Even so, many with an art background are already getting messages from spirit baby. I remember telling a conception client that her baby is into art and hopefully she is making art. The client said she was an artist who paints. Psychic artistry can be a healing and profoundly supportive mode of spirit baby communication for developing a deeper relationship.

Conception communication with spirit baby: Mom, "let's do art together." What does this mean? Mom confirms that she made a vision board. Spirit baby is confirming that "I am communicating with you."

Pregnancy communication with baby: Mom, "I want you to paint trees." What does this mean? Mom confirmed that she literally painted a tree the other day. Spirit baby is confirming that "I am helping you."

NIGHTTIME DREAMING COMMUNICATION

What is nighttime dreaming communication?

Nighttime dreaming communication involves receiving messages from spirit baby in your dreams when you are sleeping. It begins with an intention as well as an invitation to the baby spirit as you're falling asleep. The dream space is a very mysterious and powerful place that has a lot to teach us and ways to guide us. I have discovered that spirit baby communication in the dream world encompasses many different experiences with all kinds of dreams to have.

Often when your spirit baby comes into the dream space, there are a lot of questions. Is it real or is it my imagination? That is a very common response. I have discovered that when one is in communication with one's spirit baby in the dream realm, it is a very unique and specific frequency that moves through you. What I mean is that you know the dream is connected to the communication of your baby. You may doubt it for a moment or trust it so much. Creating spirit-baby communication dreaming depends on your own psychic dream awareness when you go to sleep and are having rest.

To develop dream-space spirit baby communication, try the following:

Dream Communication Method/Exercise

1. Every night before bed, make a calming pre-bed connection with your body.

2. Tell your higher self through prayer or intention that you are ready to receive your baby being to your dream space.

3. Communicate to your spirit baby that you want to meet and wish to receive a message during the night.

4. After you speak to your baby, go to sleep.

5. Let dream communication come to you and keep trying every night to see what comes. Try not to be discouraged if it doesn't come right away.

6. In the morning, write about what came through when your spirit baby does join you in the dream space.

Your Bedtime Spirit Baby Mantras

- Create with your higher self a calming personal prayer or intention.

- Share some words, such as: *Hello Spirit Baby, I am here, I am receiving, and we are connected.*

- *I would love to connect with you in my dreams and I invite you to visit me there.*

Remember, dreaming is connected with you and your baby or babies. Feel into the prophetic or more precognitive dreams and allow yourself to tap into new timelines of future knowing. Dream communication works best with deep rest, creating your practice before bed, and waking to remember the dreams.

Conception communication with spirit baby: Mom, "I visit you in your dreams." What does this mean? Mom confirms that she had a dream the other night about a girl. Spirit baby is confirming that "I am here."

Pregnancy communication with baby: Mom, "I visit you in your dreams." What does this mean? Mom confirms that she had a dream the other night about her boy. Baby is confirming that "it is me and not your imagination."

To Sum It Up…

You get to understand how many different methods exist to your spirit baby communication practices in the example and practices above.

Spirit baby communication will come to you in many ways that may be new to you, or it could be something you have already been in connection with. Keep listening and trust your love connections with spirit baby communication. Remember to have fun, soften in your heart space, laugh in playful energy with baby, and experiment. See how your intuition guides you.

When you teach yourself some of these approaches, it will support your personal connection with spirit baby. Your practice can involve all or some of the methods of communication using:

- color
- animals and insects
- numbers and symbols
- journaling and writing
- dance and movement
- music and sound
- art
- nighttime dreaming.

Aim toward trusting your free-flowing intuition and becoming more familiar with these methods. Let yourself receive and create moving forward.

Meditation Practices for Spirit Baby Communication

Here are some practical helpful and healing meditations that I have created. Using my own frequency and energetic connection within the realms of mystery and spirit baby communication. You can be a beginner / amateur or more advanced in your meditative practices. I have created these specific meditations to meet your specific heart- light with your own ability to create a relationship with spirit baby or babies. So don't stress and just please relax and tune inward to the music and my voice.

PRACTICES WITH SPIRIT BABY COMMUNICATION

Spirit Baby Meadow Meditation - Visualization

- Find a quiet, safe space and sit comfortably.
- Close your eyes and align your spine.

- Starting at the top of your head, you'll be moving your awareness slowly down. Check in with yourself first by saying hello to your head and neck. Farther down, say hello to your upper mid-body (chest), then to your breath and lungs, and onto your belly.

- Keep going downward into your lower back and hips saying hello. Then to your legs and feet.

- Create your personal love statement and let this guide you: *I am ready to communicate with you, my baby. We are love, We are light, and We are joy.*

- I want you now to access your visual space and that involves you using your mind and imagination.

- I call this next part the "Meadow Meditation."

- I now want you to see yourself within your mind, and I want you to notice that you are walking through a beautiful space of grass and flowers where you see butterflies and little tree animals.

- I want you to notice what you're wearing, what your clothes look like, what it feels like to be in your body. I want you to see yourself walking forward through this meadow, noticing how your emotions feel there and allowing peace and calm to come through you.

- See trees ahead and a large stump. Notice the feeling of the sun and the wind. Is it cloudy or is it cold there? See what else you notice in this space.

- I want you to now stand next to this stump. Then look around the space you're in.

- I want you now to notice trees in the background and see a child walking towards you. That child may be a boy, or maybe it's a girl, or perhaps you're not sure.

- I want you to see this child as being around the age of three to nine years old. I want you to see how that child comes right up to you and this is your child.

- Welcome your child. Your child wants to offer you a gift, and I want you to receive that gift, whether it is a word, a phrase, or an object.

- I want you then to give this child a gift back, whatever that is at this moment. We're allowing you both to exchange energy together.

- Next, I want you to see what else your child wants to share with you in this space.

- Take your time here, ask your child for something playful, and have a playful activity together. What does your child share with you?

- After about 5 or 10 minutes of connection and playfulness, offer your child a hug, and/or a kiss, and any gesture of temporary farewell.

- I want you to feel that connection, sense it, and be with it visually, understanding that you are a part of it. That your imagination is a part of this connection.

- Now I want you to notice the child playfully skipping away and that you are still at the stump. Now walk back down the meadow. Notice the trees and flowers all around you, feeling your whole self, body and mind, as you walk back from where you started.

- Then begin to come back to your safe space, noticing your breath and opening up your eyes. Receive your connection and experience.

- Trust it, know it, allow it to be real and present in your mind and in your intention, prayers, and mantras.

- Remember that using your imagination is going to be extremely valuable with Spirit Baby Communication and that the imagination is not wishful thinking or fantasy.

- You are having a real, true Spirit Baby Communication experience, and it is up to you to accept it and build trust with it.

MEDITATION - AUDIO Version

Direct Link: https://www.newearthchildren.com/meditationnotes-from-spiritbaby

QR Code:

You have completed your spirit baby communication meditation. This is the first of others in the next chapters for you to explore. Give yourself gratitude and allow yourself to receive that you are doing it and building continuous trust and that you are being heard and allow your own experience to unfold right before you. Remember that meditation is never about perfection. It is normal to feel like your mind is jumping around and just come back to your heart and your communication practice. I know you are in deep love and power with your spirit baby or babies so keep your heart full and let the love guide you.

CHAPTER SIX

Conscious Conception – A Star Is Welcomed

"...You are a spectacular creature and you are beautifully built. You have been specifically designed to be a creatress, a bearer of our species, and to be powerful in the most feminine of ways. You carry within the space of womb the Light of the World, which you birth anew every morning when you open your eyes. Your very existence makes the world lovelier."

~ Renèe Starr, You Are Woman, You Are Divine

He is joyful and smiles a lot, with chunky cheeks and thin, short brown hair, and she is wild and outgoing, with her long brown hair and sweet eyes. They are twins or siblings who have much to share with their parents. They share about paying attention to animals and flowers to receive messages that will come in different ways and at different times.

Conception truly is magic. The magic we know is not just from growing babies or cuddling those amazing newborns, but before – way back to the start from the inside before birth. It has been seen with the eyes and documented and confirmed that light sparks when the ovum and sperm unite. Actually, light is activated. It is pretty incredible to sit with and think about. It is a natural synergistic and electrifying dance of a force that creates together. The results are life is formed and development begins.

I remember when I conceived my children, who I birthed when I was 36 and 41 years old. My firstborn son, Rain, began with the intention that I was ready for motherhood. But I am not going to pretend that I was not terrified and fearful for many reasons, including the pregnancy, the birth, and raising a child. I decided not to fight my thoughts and worries so I could be available to become a mother, even if I was not sure of what would happen next. My wish was that I could receive conception, and I hoped our egg and sperm knew what they needed to do and that my spirit baby was ready for us. The reality was that he was ready and knew what to do because after eight months of trying, Rain was conceived. I had certain energies that came to me in the first week of early pregnancy. It felt like I was a mother before I took the test, and I even laughed about how strange it was that I had a visceral experience in my body and mind about this. I did not have any other psychic messages besides waking up at 3 am feeling starved and other body discomforts that seemed off. Still, my physical cues were unmistakable. I waited four weeks to check and confirm my pregnancy with a stick pee test. I knew patience was important, and this shaped the energy of who I was becoming and what I needed to be – open and soft to let go and just receive.

My second son Forest, born five and a half years later, was a very different experience. I was already deep into being a Spirit Baby Medium and supporting fertility energies a lot. I had been thinking, *One and done* because I was again fearful and healing big things. Forest came two months after we began to try to conceive when I was 40. He was waiting for us, and I was not sure when and if I would be ready again. Letting go of the fear was going to take time, but I knew I had conceived him. My husband and I laughed that we had conception sex the night we conceived our second son. This was because something energetically and powerfully different was experienced in the room and in our awareness of it. After a week, I could feel my body change and I had a psychic message come through. As I was cooking dinner, I saw this image come into my mind of a baby embryo cuddling in my uterus. It made my eyes water because it was emotional and truthful. I was surprised that he or I thought she sent me this message. You would think that message reassured me, but I questioned if it was a present or a future psychic prediction. It is easy for our minds to keep us in self-sabotage and questioning over trusting and allowing. I even did the pee stick test for pregnancy like the first time, but this time it said I was not pregnant. I was confused and thought, *Let me wait.* My energy said yes, but my biology test said no. I decided to wait three weeks more and retest. Well, I was pregnant and knew I was even when it said I was not on the stick test.

What can be said about conception? It is an amazing way to bring life into the body of the spirit baby. What beautiful insights and questions do you have about it? Are there any true answers available to our spiritually curious minds? Do you know how to listen to your own conception, creating a fertile field of energy in body and mind?

Hopefully, this chapter and the questions I present later will ignite some curiosity and excite you. To have curiosity, I feel, is an energy that opens us up and allows new things inward. It's not about trying to figure it all out, but just receiving the experience. At the same time, it's about allowing the excitement of what you are about to receive in so many ways into your life.

Science Is Not Spirituality

Science feels important for people in conception because a biological event is happening. The mind of science is a needed foundational place to jump from with its ideas, theories, testing data, and changing facts. Yet there are still some very real unknown parts to it all. I feel that spirit and/or soul can not be quantified or rationalized because it is an experience that is personal and abstract. Science and spirit can share space and become something, though, and they are brought together in conception. I feel that a spiritual conception can involve science, but putting it into action is a sacred responsibility and a highly intuitive experience to own. It takes true courage and inner wisdom. After all, it is significant to know that each person has biological and energetic knowledge through cells and nature to be in co-creation with life, even with confusion and many unknowns.

I want to relieve you of any extra stress on a natural conception because conception does not always have to be with positivity and with daily celebration. Actually, many babies are conceived under stress and, at other times, by accident. Consciously conceiving is about showing up for you, your partner, and your baby. It is about reflection on what it means to become a parent and that includes the good, the bad, and the ugly of it all.

You are aware of conceiving and creating ways to explore and heal. So get ready to welcome and state that you are in conscious conception. It will require little mental effort with more focus on a higher level of awareness and psychic openings. The human species is more than just a simple carbon body of cells, but a conscious force of thinking, discovering, solving, and creating. You got this!

Your conscious conception includes many practices, especially with spirit baby communication. This begins in the pre-conception or Trying to Conceive/TTC phase. Conscious conception is being fully present with your whole self upon the journey in body, mind, and spirit. It involves exploring the past, present, and future of becoming a mother or father. It is about self-exploration and having conversations with yourself and your partner, if in partnership, about life as a family and your own experiences as a child into where you are today.

Things to explore include:

- how you were raised,
- raising your future child or children,
- reflections,
- sharing values and morals,
- responsibilities, and
- raising children in this time.

This is a time of dreaming together and being open to healing the wounds of the inner child or the traumas of the past in order to grow into present parents. The list goes on in what it means and takes to consciously conceive and to call your spirit child into being with you and your family.

Conscious conception holds no specific rules and moves with a natural journey of conception or a supportive journey using extra help like Assisted Reproductive Technologies (ART). Most important is that it begins with a consciously conceiving attitude to develop into a spiritual exploration to expand into what guides you.

Your spirit baby consciousness is being activated through your own contemplations that involve more private intimate practices with spirit baby in many ways. Remembering your style of communication will lead you into better ways into communication that can easily open the heart to more discovery and ease into motherhood and/or fatherhood.

What Spirit Babies Want from Parents

Spirit babies want love and connection. Could it be that simple to create life and do it for companionship and love? Life would be really boring without amazing little babies growing into children to share it with... don't you think? We cannot have all the answers, nor can we control conception, no matter how hard technology tries. Some things are not about force or controlling outcomes.

Can you accept that you are a guardian to your child or children who are born into this time for their life experience with you? I often say that we do not own our child/children, and they are borrowed to be loved and cared for. So be open to their own mission in this world.

Each parent is unique to the creation of a family. Spirit baby communication is not reserved for just mothers only. Fathers are also included, and my husband had dreams of our son. That was his way into communication. My husband found his own way with our future children. I have supported many couples and men individually. Just like single moms and other parenting dynamics that are all in alignment.

PARTNERSHIP

> *"Connecting with their children before conception may be an aspect of fatherhood that men are ready to rediscover. It is an idea with the most ancient echoes: some Australian Aboriginal people are said to believe that conception involves the father's going into the spiritual realm, the 'Dreamtime,' and meeting there the soul of his future child."*
>
> ~Elisabeth Hallett, Soul Trek: Meeting Our Children on the Way to Birth

Consider these questions:

- What will conception bring you next?
- What does your spirit baby communication relationship look like?
- Do you feel like you're winning or failing?
- How does your partner communicate?
- Do they need guidance from you or outside of you?
- Does your conception feel lonely and without the energy of your partner?
- Or do you feel fully held by your partnership?

Conscious Conception and Fathers

Spirit baby is not only about the mother and her own lineage and story of conception into pregnancy. If you are in a partnership with a male, it also is about the father and his lineage and story for conception. I'll point out also that conception is not just about heterosexual couples, but also lesbian and gay couples and single mothers by choice, which I mentioned in the introduction, but do not go into it any further as it is not my area of expertise.

I have supported many couples in private spirit baby sessions. What I've noticed with most of the masculine partners is that they must be open to connect with the psychic information and understand their own heart space for self-healing. It is not about being super logical or analytical when connecting with spirituality and spirit baby communication. It is actually about ease, inwardness, and reflective openings. I notice that I work well with these kinds of masculine thinking energies because I can help with better listening and understanding to support the partner, whether women or men. I have supported lawyers, doctors, engineers, musicians, and artists. Not that the male partner needs to be any of those, but the father-to-be thought process is easy to work with. I encourage partners to support each other with communication and open dialogue to explore parenting with spirit baby. Not every partner has a strong psychic connection, but that doesn't matter. It's really just an openness and availability to show up that is the most important, I feel.

Partnership often has nothing to do with the mother's inability to conceive solely on her own energy, but the energy of the father and his journey towards awakening. You may not be happy to hear this because maybe it feels like it's out of your control. But it is so important that you two feel a connection and go into deep communication together in a partnership. You want to be able to hold everybody's energy accountable for creation, as your child wants that from you.

Spirit baby conception communication meditation is a very unique and heart opening experience. In a conception meditation you get to trust and call upon the energies around you that are meant to guide and support you.

PRACTICES WITH SPIRIT BABY COMMUNICATION

Sensing & Feeling with Spirit Baby Communication

- Find a quiet space and sit comfortably.

- Close your eyes, align your spine, and feel your whole body.

- Starting at the top of your head, you'll be moving your awareness slowly down. Check in with yourself first by saying hello to your head and neck. Farther down, say hello to your upper mid-body (chest), then to your breath and lungs, and onto your belly.

- Keep going downward into your lower back and hips saying hello. Then to your legs and feet.

- Let your body's check-in create an open space of ease and relaxation.

- Next, bring your attention to your heart and listen to your spiritual heart center.

- Allow your intention to sense your spirit baby is here now.

- Trust it, know it, allow it to be real and present in your mind, and in your intention, prayers, and mantras.

- Share a personal love statement from your heart and let this example guide you: *Hello my baby being, I am listening. I am here. I am ready. I love you. I trust our loving connections.* (Remember, you are elevating your energy.)

- Sense your spirit baby and allow your open, sensing intuitive self to connect with feelings. Let your emotions and other sensations guide you.

- Sit with that energy of you and spirit baby. Keep having a conversation from the heart.

- Sit with your breath and trust that you are being heard and received.

- When you feel complete after 10 to 20 minutes, then end your meditation with prayer or an intention of gratitude and love.

- Come back to your quiet space of meditation by sensing and feeling the energy of your spirit baby or babies.

Spirit Baby Communication – Partnership with Spirit Baby

- Find a quiet space and sit comfortably.

- Close your eyes, align your spine, and feel your whole body.

- Starting at the top of your head, you'll be moving your awareness slowly down. Check in with yourself first by saying hello to your head and neck. Farther down, say hello to your upper mid-body (chest), then to your breath and lungs, and onto your belly.

- Keep going downward into your lower back and hips saying hello. Then to your legs and feet.

- Let your body's check-in create an open space of ease and relaxation.

- Next, bring your attention to your heart and listen to your spiritual heart center.

- Allow your intention to sense your spirit baby is here now.

- Share a personal love statement from your heart and let this example guide you: *Hello my baby being, I am ready. I am grateful to receive you. I love you. I trust our loving connections.*

- Sit with that energy of you and spirit baby.

- After you've created your personal connection with Spirit baby being then I want you now to allow the energetic space of your partner into your heart.

- You love your partner and heart gaze together. That means allowing yourself to sit right next to you or right before you and feel each other's presence and heart.

- I want you to intend or imagine that your spirit baby being is sitting between both of you.

- I want you to see how your heart links like a glow and light from your heart to your baby's heart and to your partner's heart. You are all receiving heart communication and the frequency of love.

- Your baby is sharing a message. What is it? Let yourself see or hear or feel it.

- When you feel complete after 10 to 20 minutes, then end your meditation with prayer or an intention of gratitude and love.

MEDITATION - AUDIO Version

Direct Link: https://www.newearthchildren.com/meditationnotes-from-spiritbaby

QR Code:

CHAPTER SEVEN

Infertility – Surrendering Into Healing

"There is a power in surrender. It is a state that is imbued with a feeling of trust, brought to life by some sense of faith in the divine intelligence that runs our life."

~ **Michelle Oravitz, The Way of Fertility: Awaken Your Reproductive Potential Through the Power of Ancient Wisdom**

She is beautiful and expansive with short, dark, thick hair and penetrating brown eyes. She shares her mission of being a powerful changer for her mother and humanity. She is cheering her mother on to heal her past, open to the freedom of emotional expression, and let go of how she will come into creation. She is ready!

My experience with infertility in my own body is none. I am not going to pretend to have an understanding of a personal experience with infertility because I do not. The majority of the support I offer with spirit baby communication for over a decade has been focused on women and men, and I have connected with many energy fields to provide healing, answers, and inspiration for dealing with infertility, both with known and unknown causes.

What I understand is that I have been called into this specific area for children before life without any attachment or triggers held personally. I get to create possibilities and an openness of co-creative knowledge for others in an unbelievable felt sense, and real ways. My heart goes out to you if you struggle with conception because infertility is a loss, and that grief deserves recognition, space to be with, and love for how to serve and heal with it. I will not minimize an experience that is taxing and presents many protocols and interventions. I want you to know that I see you. I hear you. I am here for you. I love you.

Conception can seem like a simple experience, but it is not for many. It does not always work to naturally conceive, and it can be a deeply brutal and heart-invoking experience with many unknown parts and fears. No one is ever prepared to experience infertility and the obstacles and challenges that come with it. The hardest part is trusting and listening to how to create and support your own conception into pregnancy. No one can promise or guarantee an outcome but you and baby or babies. I have great empathy for those who struggle to become a mother and/or a father. It can feel unfair, confusing, disappointing, rageful, and, of course, deeply emotional.

Where Are You, Spirit Baby?

Why Can I Not Conceive?

Infertility is not about bargaining with God or punishment. Nor is it meant to be or not meant to be New-Age or spiritual self-help wrongdoings or ideas. Infertility is not a disease or a label to be branded by, but it is understandable why it does feel that way. Not knowing or having solid reasons for the lack of becoming pregnant brings up many feelings and thoughts.

I do believe infertility is never about giving up because it can be temporary. Working towards a creative conception into parenthood is a timeline that can exist. The journey of conceiving may not be revealed right away. Each person has to find their way toward healing and creation. This is not a simple and easy healing for many women and men who have been pushed towards this path for many known and unknown reasons.

Infertility is not new. It has been a part of history for centuries, depicted in drawings on rocks and walls, literature, and shared through the passing of stories in cultures and societies around the globe. It was more mysterious until medical science was able to study and test fertility. Infertility has been known as "A Woman's Burden," but it no longer needs to be a women's issue. Actually, male infertility has grown over the years with male factors as issues in conceiving.

Cultures have different experiences within infertility, using rituals that follow generations of cultural traditions. In their book, *Chumash Healing: Changing Health and Medical Practices in an American Indian Society,* noted that: the Northern California Indians used baby rocks that were meant to cure sterility. The couples would be sent these rocks and a prayer for fertility would be made. Other nature based earth rituals of powder and paste would be used to further good energy towards fertility.

So What Is the Holdup to Receive Conception and Pregnancy?

Is My Spirit Baby Mad or Upset?

Your spirit baby is not punishing you, taunting you, or purposely creating fear in you because you did something specific to cause a wanted experience of motherhood and/or fatherhood. There are many reasons outside of biology for infertility, and it may be the hardest part of the conception journey that needs healing. You will feel and experience the challenges of infertility, and you will need to remember to stay calm and connected. Bring your inner self and awareness to this mission. It is not just about you and your partner (if in partnership), but also about your child or children. The unique lessons in the infertility journey will be revealed and unfold throughout it. It is a time, if this is your experience, to drop deeply inward and that includes surrendering and remembering your love. I know you can be an alchemist to the hardship and create something powerful and new from it. I truly feel this to be true for you.

You are the leader in your intuitive conception, and you are the advocate for you. This is especially true if you are using a fertility clinic for support or have been trying all the programs, diets, and workshops with nothing changing your outcome. It can be easy to get caught up in what others tell you, such as social media ads, other fertility practitioners, and even fertility doctors. I am not saying to ignore your doctor, but self-trust is more attuned and accurate than going along with procedures and information that may not pertain to your personal fertility story and struggle.

I have heard women say, "I went to the fertility clinic and all they offered me was a bunch of horrible low numbers and impossible stats. How am I supposed to trust conception and spirit baby connections with multiple issues and diagnoses?" Well, it will not be easy, and most likely it will be hard to trust how to continue forward with guidance. It can be impossible at times to trust, but I want to offer you insights so you can claim your purpose of motherhood and move into your intuitive presence.

Remember, it's not about minimizing the information you get from the clinic or doctor, who may have your best interests in supporting your conception. But they do not hold all the power or all the answers or solutions to what works for you. It is more about empowering yourself to listen, make choices, and move forward. Many issues can be tested. Maybe the fertility doctor told you that your endometriosis is bad, you have low ovarian reserve, your uterus is stubborn and lazy, or your fallopian tubes are clogged or scarred, you have an autoimmune disorder, you have only one ovary, your eggs are old or bad, the sperm is old or bad, or you're just too old. So what! I have seen all these issues and guess what? Babies were conceived and born healthy, often naturally, and beautifully. With "so what," I am not saying to deny your personal medical issues that are a real and serious problem. But not everything that is off balance in your body is incurable nor just a physical issue to cure.

The fertility obstacles are asking for you to navigate through them and explore what your own personal healing becomes. It will ask you to get creative. I have heard and seen the hearts of many women and men asking for the WHY and HOW, while also knowing that parenthood is MEANT TO BE. That is not false thought, imagination, or desire. The truth your heart is telling you, outside of your mind, is you are meant to be a parent. You are listening to the call, and as you agree to the call, it will be with the theme of fertility healing. You can continue to prepare your physical body, emotional and mental wellness, and energetic spiritual field to match your frequency with your child. I highly encourage you to keep preparing. Know that this does not mean the effort will be without days that feel discouraging or are filled with anger or deep sorrow. You will also have days of hope, inspiration, and motivation!

I have seen the impossible become a possibility. No one can tell anyone what they know to be true to the heart of the journey to be a falsehood. It can take months to years to bring a child into your world, but it is possible and may come in surprising ways. I see it all the time through birth announcements mailed to me, emails of gratitude, and meeting some spirit babies in their bodies upon Earth. It is pretty awesome.

What about IVF/IUI or Other Interventions?

What Does Spirit Baby Feel About That?

Do They Want to Come This Way or Not?

Sometimes intervention is the only path. IVF and IUI are common interventions when pregnancy is not happening or single or multiple miscarriages are experienced. To give you a better understanding, I will explain what these interventions are and you can do more research.

IVF is also known as "in vitro fertilization." IVF can be a complex process that involves egg retrieval, and combining egg and sperm for fertilization, with the hopes of creating a healthy embryo or embryos to later transfer into the uterus and grow a baby.

Another intervention is IUI, which is also known as "intrauterine insemination" or "artificial insemination." It is when sperm cells are directly put into the uterus during ovulation to help them get closer to the egg for conception. IUI is often done by doctors and midwives in a clinical setting. ICI, "intracervical insemination," is when sperm is inserted into the cervix, which is not far into the uterus like in IUI. IUI and ICI are similar, but ICI can be done at home without medical doctors or clinic support. IUI can be done by oneself using devices from medical supply stores or other specific already-made tools for this intervention.

Other options could include, but are not limited to:

- the use of medications and injections,
- using other sources for becoming a parent, such as:
  - embryo adoption
  - sperm donation
  - surrogacy, and/or
  - child adoption

Technology can be super supportive, but it also can be abused and not necessary. It is never an easy choice or decision to use intervention because most spiritual women want a natural conception and pregnancy into birth. However, that is not always how it goes. I like to call the use of any kind of intervention "Creative Conception." A Creative Conception is getting creative with ways of untraditional conception and that may be the only way your baby or babies are coming to be born earthside. There are a lot of emotions and feelings to process when having to use interventions, especially with more simpler interventions to higher, risker interventions.

How does spirit baby communication work with IVF or IUI?

Spirit baby communication works no matter what kind of conception you are getting ready for. This means you can have a spiritual conception through your Creative Conception. I have supported so many women and couples within IVF and IUI conceptions and it is not hard or completed. You can and will do it because you are learning and healing along the way from infertile to fertile.

Why can't baby tell me if they want to be born through IVF or IUI, or not?

I believe spirit baby can guide you and tell you if this is the way your baby will be conceived. It is wise to ask and then be open to listening to yourself and baby. Listen for whether to take action or to wait. It may not be that easy and simple for some. Sometimes one must have patience and spiritual connection. Some babies are not meant to tell you what you need to conceive them, but I will not tell you not to ask. Sometimes the journey itself needs space to sit with so it can unfold regarding what comes

next. Even though you may not have received an answer from spirit baby, you might feel ready to move forward with using an intervention. I have personally experienced spirit babies who have shared that they either will come through IVF only, they will not come through IVF, or they're completely neutral with coming through naturally or IVF.

Not everyone gets the immediate answers, especially if the healing has layers with current/past childhood experiences, past-lives issues, or ancestral trauma or other multidimensionality upgrades. The deeper reason or need to wait to be born can be a mystery, but do not let that shift your mission to motherhood and/or fatherhood. The healing is about more than conception and pregnancy, and you're being led by intuition and love to find it all out.

Possible Reasons for the Delay or Divine Timing

Below is a list of reasons I have heard spirit babies and the spirit of the parent's own energy share. Remember that our children have their own lessons to activate and contribute.

I am going to share what I have witnessed through supporting others:

- The <u>current timeline</u> of your life is active with unresolved trauma.

- The issues are connected to <u>your specific</u> childhood, lineage/ancestral trauma and past.

- The issues are connected to <u>your partner's</u> childhood, lineage/ancestral trauma and past.

- The issues are a <u>past life</u> that is active in the current timeline of healing.

- The issues are <u>spiritual</u>: involving multidimensional/galactic realms/other realities.

- The issues are connected to the <u>spirit of your child</u>: related to the above list.

I am sorry that you are struggling and experiencing disappointment, pain, and suffering. Your conception or infertility is not about victimization or self- blaming. Your life is not meant to be childless or filled with suffering and confusion. I believe in you and the many women who have come into my sacred sessions over the many years. I have seen infertility, and I experienced supporting and listening to women taking back their power in the fertility experience. You are made to create and hold this energy of life into possibility. Let spirit baby be your guiding force of light, move into new heart practices, and get your clarity. If you feel super-stressed and sense that you cannot do it, then please hit the pause button. Reset yourself and begin to construct a new path forward.

Spirit Baby Whispers Secrets to Heal Your Communication

Infertility is not a new issue, and it has been in existence since the beginning of humankind some would believe. However, what has occurred is that more and more people are sharing the struggle – the lack of being able to conceive naturally, waiting three to seven or more years to conceive through natural means or interventions.

Infertility is a personal issue that is often misdiagnosed because many who are tagged or labeled as infertile have become pregnant. I believe infertility can be temporary, and this depends on the person. It also depends on the partner. Infertility is always connected to the past because right now, in this moment, you are whole. Your energy is creation, and the past holds old issues, like a weight that feels slow or immovable.

What does spirit baby say about infertility?

Infertility is what we come up with to figure out why people were not conceiving, but remember it is a temporary illusion or issue. The label of infertility is NOT just a "fix it and therefore it is all figured out" situation because it is not supposed to be just like most life experiences. It is a multileveled experience that deserves a specific connection, and the reasons and healings will vary. When coming from a place of a wider view, then you get to build energy around healing and move in new and changing ways. For example,

I speak a lot about fertility and conception on *Spirit Baby Radio*, a podcast with over 190 episodes. The episodes go into deeper spirit baby conversations with emotional and spiritual tones of healing, self-awareness, and intuition insights for the journey into motherhood.

Most conversations in my sessions and those shared on *Spirit Baby Radio* podcast are within the lack of conception and issue and the healing of miscarriage and grief and fear. I have sensed, felt, and seen from the spirit of the parent or parents in an energetic body field the messages from the spirit of baby or babies. I could never say infertility is one thing to solve. It takes dropping deeply inward and releasing the mental energy that holds you and doing the self-work being asked of you. It is your responsibility to open with it and allow leadership of the heart to teach and guide.

A fertility journey is unique to the individual and not everyone has the same issues. Fertility clinics all have varying opinions in their methods and something to understand and explore. Some clinics will have high success rates, while others may fail greatly at it, for you.

I have seen infertility change the lives of mothers and fathers in ways towards awakening and growing into healing major life issues. As I've said before, it's not going to be easy. But you get to be the Alchemist of your experience of infertility, into fertility, into pregnancy, and into parenthood. We have to remember that everything is connected to energy, and that is not meant to minimize real true experiences of struggle and difficult challenges. Remember that your personal journey and mission into motherhood is going to require a lot of you at times. Other times you will just flow on the path towards it. Offering encouragement is the biggest thing that I share, and also setting an intention of preparation. You are preparing. When you are preparing, you are focused, open, and intuitive. You are moving with forward energy into a timeline of creation so you can learn, grow, and enjoy life together with your baby.

What does spirit baby need from you within infertility?

Spirit baby is an energy that is real, and spirit baby lives in a different place of energies and frequencies. It is easy to hold our limited human-minded ideas, thoughts, and more about this. I encourage spirit baby communication for these reasons because it can be a powerful guiding tool toward parenthood. Remember that your connection is built in different ways, including but not limited to meditations that are movement-based, visual, and feeling-oriented. The spirit baby relationship can include loving spirit baby intentions, healing mantras, empowering affirmations, artistic vision boards, other creative muses, projects of spirit baby love letters, nature adventures outdoors, and more.

How Do I Know My Spirit Baby Is in Communication with the Fertility Journey?

I know it is hard to understand at times, but I really trust that your spirit baby or babies are in communication with you, speaking with you, and sharing messages of support and guidance. The missing part of the conversation and often overlooked is:

- "Are you listening?"
- "Do you believe it?"
- "Do you trust it?
- "Are you open to it?"

- "Are you too much in your head to recognize your connection?"

- "What do you specifically need for your connection?"

I wish I could just offer you the secret formula and the answers all in one conversation, but I cannot and I don't think it's meant to be that way. It is not easy for many to let go and surrender outside of the mind. I promise your quest into motherhood/fatherhood is not a waste of time, nor is it over.

Infertility and the Use of Intervention with Spirit Baby Communication

Spirit baby communication within the use of IVF can deeply support the needed healing space. I feel, with IVF, it is important to take it slow with the next steps. Work with self-awareness, self-care, and self-love to allow more time for listening, getting guidance, and utilizing proper information regarding your consent. Your most important resource in the whole IVF journey will be intuition. What I recommend to those doing or feeling called to IVF is to move mindfully and heartfully. In that one can allow decisions and choices to be made without a rush or making fear-based decisions and taking actions that can easily result in emotional and mental exhaustion and the risk of damage and needed repair.

IVF is not just about the science of chemistry and biology. A physical opportunity with an embryo or embryos does not always result in conception into pregnancy, as we know. It is important to do emotional and spiritual work around the journey for greater success of receiving life. Each step in the IVF journey has a need and that means preparing for pregnancy, rituals with stimulation and retrieval, meditations before embryo transfer, and healing energy after transfer. IVF needs space for creating rituals with the body, as well as the body of energy that it receives before the physical body does, which is why preparing spiritually and psychologically is beneficial on many levels.

Beautiful Rituals: For Retrieval, Embryos & Transfers

- **A Retrieval Ritual** can include prayers, mantras, and intentions. In preparation, anoint the body with love, whether it's external physical and/or emotional and spiritual energies. Allow yourself to experience you as a Divine Light that has healthy, abundant follicles to share. Allow yourself to go into the retrieval with healing love and compassion. After the procedure, make sure to send beautiful light to your eggs, and wait for the sperm to meet them with an excitement of joy and love.

- **As egg and sperm meet in their most beautiful biological space,** you are going to open your heart. You're going to allow light energy into the heart space as they are merging together. Send a prayer that they are healthy, and that you are receiving them with synergy to feel, sense, and know them as a part of your body.

- **Take it easy and allow yourself to dream and be with the imagery of pregnancy.** Listen to your intuitive self, and don't wait to trust that you will be pregnant. That you are receiving the timeline of pregnancy, and that your body is in chemical, energetic synergy with embryos fully activated and ready.

Why do some souls come through IVF?

I can only offer you what spirit babies have shared with me. Some babies do not want to be born through IVF, and I am sorry to say that but it is true. I never discourage the path of the parent unless the message is super strong to not explore IVF. I find many fertility clinics go quickly to IVF based on non-medical factors, assumptions about age, or guesswork about poor egg quality without checking it. Age is on the list, but it is not the final determinator of conception. Healthy women can conceive over 35.

IVF should never be taken lightly. For many reasons, it brings up many feelings for a woman trying to conceive. Adoption can be very triggering, but this energy can offer a new connection and a way to create. It is easily misinterpreted as the only option and that is not true. It can create opportunity that opens up new energy and possibility. So never leave adoption out, whether it be a gestational carrier, embryo adoption, or baby/child adoption. This is a time to go deeper and welcome change and investigate.

PRACTICES WITH SPIRIT BABY COMMUNICATION

Spirit Baby Communication Practice – Sacred Embryonic Vibration

- Find a quiet space and sit comfortably.

- Close your eyes, align your spine, and feel your whole body.

- Starting at the top of your head, you'll be moving your awareness slowly down. Check in with yourself first by saying hello to your head and neck. Farther down, say hello to your upper mid-body (chest), then to your breath and lungs, and onto your belly.

- Keep going downward into your lower back and hips saying hello. Then to your legs and feet.

- Let your body's check-in create an open space of ease and relaxation.

- Next, bring your attention to your heart and listen to your spiritual heart center.

- Allow your visual and sensing self to see and bring your embryo into your heart.

- Take your hands and place them over your heart.

- Experience a deep knowing that your embryo(s) are being integrated into your heart. (That is where conception begins - in the heart chakra).

- I want you to experience this opalescent soft pastel rainbow vibe within the embryo(s).

- Bring your hands from your heart down upon your abdomen or womb.

- Rest your hands and bring your embryo(s) baby(ies) into your womb.

- Let your breath be easeful and your body be receiving.

- Your embryo(s) are synergy with your uterus and your body is fruitful and baby snuggle up into pregnancy.

- Share a personal love statement from your heart and let this example guide you: *Hello my baby being, I am ready. I am grateful to receive you. I love you. I am here.*

- Sit with your breath and trust that you are being heard and received.

- When you feel complete after 10 to 20 minutes, then end your meditation with prayer or an intention of gratitude and love.

MEDITATION - AUDIO Version

Direct Link:
https://www.newearthchildren.com/meditationnotes-from-spiritbaby

QR Code:

SCAN ME

CHAPTER EIGHT

Pregnancy – A Pre-Birth Communication Experience

"The star children are not a curiosity, just a normal part of our evolutionary process. They are the front-runners of other, even more intellectually advanced beings. We must give these children whatever it takes to feed their great mental capacity."

~Meg Blackburn Losey, PhD, *The Children of Now*

He has crystal blue eyes and soft hair. At 21 weeks pregnant, his mother is ready to keep connecting with him. This baby boy easily communicates throughout the pregnancy. He shares about foods he likes, how he feels, what he needs, if anything, and more. His purpose will be revealed through psychic conversations and through an Earth body experience that the whole family is welcoming.

Pregnancy is the most precious and incredible phase of life. It is an experience not given enough love and care for how pivotal and transformative it is for women becoming mothers in our times today. Pregnancy is about connecting with instincts, embodying complete trust, and moving through alignment. It is a mutual relationship between mother and baby, and the accompanying attunement keeps everybody safe and connected for the duration of pregnancy and into birthing.

After all, the baby being, whether in the first, second, or third trimester, has a connection started often before conception that is completely real and present with the mother-to-be. Communication is not just energetic, but physical and emotional. It involves the physiology of gestation, biological development, sensations, psychic realms of mind-telepathy, and other emotional energies. The mother and child relationship is a natural primal bond. This is beyond just the mechanics of the biology that is happening, and it is the most natural and beautiful part of a baby human; It is intelligence that is spiritual and organic. You can view pregnancy as a rebirth of Spring that offers the deepest healing and the most creative energies ever. It is about using less thinking, less words, and less thoughts, and instead more sentience, presence, and beingness.

Pregnancy is a human affair. That means it impacts us all. It is not just about becoming a mother, but also for the partner, family, friends, and community. Basically, the energy of life is the most valuable gift to share with all of humanity. Have you ever noticed how pregnant women have a glow? Do you notice pregnant mothers? Are you looking at them with reverence and honor? If not, you should stop, notice, and experience this. When you notice a pregnant woman, say a prayer in your heart and hold love for them because the experience is sacred. That baby spark is already sharing so much more than just growing inside a mother.

I have to share. *I remember curating a birth art show many years ago, where I gathered many artists who had conception-, pregnancy- and birth-inspired art pieces. One art piece, which* has the most awesome meaning, remains on my wall today above where I have sat and tuned into spirit babies for years in private sessions in Topanga, California. The artist told me how she was inspired to create it. A class project was to create something that was the most precious thing in the world. Everyone was creating paintings and sculptures of money. She made a woman covered in gems and crystals with violet light and darkness around her. In the center of the painting are her hands wrapped around her belly, like a frame with the baby inside her body as the center. The woman is in a breech position. You could see the baby inside, like the painting is an x-ray through the body. The artist truly captured the most valuable "thing," which was more than just a thing or material object. The most valuable thing is human life. The artist created this image so beautifully. The meaning of it will always be in my heart and a story I love to share.

How do you create a sacred and spiritual pregnancy with pre-birth communication?

You must first self-reflect and sit with the sacredness of conception into pregnancy and birth. Pregnancy is meant to be worshiped with adoration, care, and love. It is a truly magical gift and, for a mother, it is literally why you exist. Your pregnancy will be your own and an experience that will ask you to be present, tuned in, and available. You will want to be available for physical, emotional, mental, and spiritual care. It will be a wild adventure of positive moments and tiresome negative moments. Your purpose is to show up with a spiritually aligned connection to yourself and your baby. It is a time to allow your baby to be your guiding light over the weeks and months of development. You are both working to support each other, and your intuitive strength will help you bond and connect along the way. At last, you will arrive at the final and very important part of pregnancy – labor and birth – and you will prepare to meet your baby earthside.

What will the future of pregnancy be like? What is your responsibility for raising a New Earth Child/Children?

Pregnancy in today's world is a completely different experience than it was back in a time when nature was respected and pregnancy was allowed to be a natural part of life through fertility and birthing. It was a time when the Earth provided whole foods that were chemical-free, and there were fewer toxicities in an environment of more ease and

lower stress. Today, a lot of competing energies – in a more toxic world of industrialization with abusive old systems in place – will play their roles within the consciousness of pregnancy overall. What I mean by that is pregnant women are not going to be encouraged to be freethinkers in societies impacted by old, outdated methods and constant fears that become normal instead of the madness that are. The media is part to blame and it is like an inoculation to sedate others with fears, negativity, and pressures. The pressures of what pregnancy is supposed to be like.

The common model and subconscious mindset is that you or your baby will die if you do not follow the birth trends that make pregnancy and birth seem like a disease or it is dangerous and needs saving. The biggest threats today in pregnancy and other areas are psychological brainwashing, mass confusion, and, of course, corruption. Birthing is an industry today, and to question and be open to your pregnancy's spiritual path will require you to advocate for yourself and create a community of support. Your pregnant body is your own, and choosing how you live inside your body and mind is your right. Your style of birthing, whether it is a free birth, home birth, center birth, or hospital birth, is your own choice, and with any choice, risk is always involved. No matter what, it is up to you to come back to your pregnancy and birthing instincts, like your ancestors did... before industrialization and the medicalization of birth. That was a time of using nature and without distraction and pollution. Something to remember is that you can come back to creating something new and natural. If you cannot and feel or have been traumatized then understand that you can and will heal. Remember to love your-self and hold compassion.

Pre-birth communication is a natural instinct that is going to save the future of children

I understand that the consciousness of birth impacts us all, and this is why pre-birth communication will keep transfiguring for inner domination to take birth back for the women, people, midwives, doulas, radical birth keepers, and free birthers. Pregnant women need to keep opening up to questions, trust intuition, understand the system, including what consent means, and advocate for themselves and their children. Creating change is an inside-and-out job. Pregnancy will bring fear, but it will also bring in love, learning, and education.

It is no surprise that the maternity health care system is in dire need of continuous improvements. Mothers and babies need to be taken care of and viewed with less fear, neglect, and intervention, and birth seen as a natural process, with less giving of personal power away. Medical doctors and nurses must be re-taught to update with the new technology of the times, but more than ever the consciousness of the people, which is literally changing and shifting every day. It is a massive reboot and re-creation of life, so the future can exist.

Dr. Bruce Lipton, a world-renowned biologist, epigenetics expert, and *Spirit Baby Radio* guest, shares that, in the way the world is going, we are in a mass extinction. The many systems we belong to hold a deeply subconscious story and it is hurting humanity. It is like many people are living in a sleep state and go through the motions of keeping the idea that pregnancy and birth are unsafe and in need of control. Also, that pregnant women need intervention with no body autonomy. The body is owned by someone else who will save the day, and if you are not helped, a "then you can die" mentality gets set in. That ongoing story is present in the minds of many, and these old beliefs need to go, such as that birth is unnatural. That is untrue and unsupportive.

We live in the perfect time to remember that pregnancy and birth are natural and normal. That pregnancy is not a danger, and mothers know how to birth babies of all shapes and sizes during all kinds of pregnancy conditions. Babies know how to come into the world with their mothers, because they were both built for it. I know many of us hold that the future will be positive, with less lies. Those fears will be erased and a new belief can surface so the energy of rapid changes can take over for our community of people, pregnant mothers, spirit babies, birth workers, birth advocates, human rights activists, and people who just care about others and life.

How do you open and create communication with your baby before birth?

What is pre-birth communication?

Pregnancy communication or pre-birth communication is a deeply available and important experience that is spiritual bonding before life and from the womb. Accessing your own instinctual ability to connect with pre-birth communication for your son or daughter is spiritual parenting from the start. You do not need to wait to parent your child after birth because it begins in pre-conception and especially during pregnancy. Your child is an existing being of cells and biology, a soul supporting her or his body, an energy or vibration, and you get to build a trusting loving relationship together. Your pregnancy and birth together is the rebirth of you. At the birth of your child into being, she or he will come into their tiny body as a newborn, and you may feel like you have known each other or waited your whole life for that moment.

Pregnancy communication can offer you many different internal messages using your psychic sense and intuition. You have an opportunity to listen and allow spiritual messages to support you. Your ability to access that natural, instinctual connection will come in many different ways as you have been guided in the earlier chapters: daydreaming, nighttime dreaming, meditation, and creative uses of music, art, and dance, along with messages of signs and symbols, and more.

Pre-birth communication offers insights to build trust with how your baby shares with you when she or he needs something from you for your health, your emotions, and your spiritual heart, and you will know it as truth. Babies can share many supportive insights by providing alerts and warnings that can be guiding for pregnancy and birth. The tricky part of receiving messages is deciphering your fear over intuition, but not to worry. That will come with your feeling safe in your body and practicing self-trust and intuition.

Remember, messages and connections are not only serious medical or alerting issues, but they can also be playful, fun, positive, and with laughs. Your baby is open to the intimate communication you both share. It is about staying in communication and paying attention to self-care, emotional wellness, and your spiritual upgrades. Remember, love is everything, and love is the energy baby is thriving on and that you are connected with.

Besides the joyful, exciting, and playful parts of pregnancy, you may experience more challenges with fear and big emotions. No one is free from fear, especially in pregnancy and in labor and birth. Pregnancy anxieties come for many reasons, and this is why creating a pre-birth communication practice can support ease and embodiment through different methods. Anxieties happen for many reasons, from miscarriage/stillbirth history, to past or current medical concerns, emotional issues, personal challenges, and more. So many changes are happening during pregnancy, and it's not always going to feel positive. Honestly, that is okay. I want to encourage you in those times of fear and anxiety to understand how to work with your emotions and healing in beautiful ways so you get the support you need. You never have to do it alone. Let pre-birth communication guide your relationship of trust and connection with your baby being.

TIPS for Moving Safely through the Stages of Pregnancy

What does 1st-trimester spirit baby communication look like?

First trimester pre-birth communication is no different than 2nd and 3rd trimester. What I have observed through private sessions is that the 1st trimester is the hardest, as the body is adjusting and emotions are high. Those high emotions can create a misinterpretation and uneasiness. Then emotions can set you up to over-question whether baby is okay and lead to other wrong ideas and thoughts. The fear of loss can falsely be created, causing more unnecessary stress. Remember that the 1st trimester is a time of recalibrating to a new body of energy, and you will need rest and more rest. So allow yourself to create with ease and heart communication. Be open, and as you move into the 2nd trimester, you will allow the shift to bring a different perspective of how you communicate. By the 3rd, you will be a pre-birth communication pro and getting ready for labor and birth.

What does 2nd-trimester spirit baby communication look like?

Your 2nd-trimester pre-birth communication practice gets to accelerate, and it will offer you new insights, personal power, and spiritual wisdom. It is very common in the 2nd trimester to feel like your body is more present in the pregnancy. You're getting used to how you communicate with your baby, and you get to expand more into different intuitive practices. Intuition can become more heightened and increase, and this is because your natural instincts are being activated and that is basic spirituality. As your intuition increases, then you get to build more trust and confidence as you're moving toward your 3rd trimester. You will continue to feel new experiences coming up and sometimes even other uneasy experiences coming up. Make sure to continue to be open and receive any telepathic connections with baby at this time, knowing and trusting that it will help prepare you for labor and birth. It is not uncommon to also feel misattuned at times. Try not to create fear around that, and instead come back to balancing out your energy so you can be in heart and mind communication with baby.

What does 3rd-trimester spirit baby communication look like?

Your 3rd trimester is about getting ready for the final show of labor into birth, which will bring up a lot of massive emotions and feelings. You will question many things about preparing for the birth, and the most important part for you is to stay in your pre-birth communication practice as you enter labor. You have to remember that you are in deep attunement with the baby that has been growing in your belly over the past months. Nobody can tell you how you feel in your body, and your baby will share with you anything that's coming up. Keep tuning in and listening as you have been with your communication. And if you have not, you can do it now!

Remember that it is about both of you and nobody else. When mothers are coming into dilation in a physiological way, I often energetically view it as a spiritual dilation. That's because the energy of the body changes from six weeks to four weeks to two weeks before actual birth. What this means is that the anxiousness, excitement, and uneasiness are part of the preparation for birth. A portal is opening and the merging of worlds is happening. Your spiritual heart and whole body are opening up, and the light already held moves more deeply. The light comes into this world as baby takes a breath after leaving the watery womb to enter the air of Earth. Pre-birth communication goes into action during labor and birthing. The baby and soul are merged and a child is born into being.

As you enter your **4th trimester** (also known as "postpartum," where you'll need specific self-care), your newborn baby is still in telepathic and psychic communication with you. You will want to follow your deepest instincts forward into motherhood.

You own your labor and you own your birth...Baby communication is available

What about birth emergencies or interventions?

How do you use pre-birth communication during a birth emergency?

What about cesarean births and pre-birth communication?

What about hospital births, center births, home births, and unassisted free births?

My intention with these questions is to create change in the energy of what we believe, what we are experiencing, and how we get to heal and move forward. I understand that this may be triggering, and, hopefully, it will help you deepen into another layer of your life of having a child.

I have had the personal experience of birthing my baby in a perceived emergency situation as a home birth transfer. I wish I could say I was treated well by the hospital, but I was not. A dangerously closed-minded system in the hospital with high cesarean rates did not like to receive transfers, especially from home births. In that mindset, the judgments of home birth are in conflict with current birth trends in society.

This first birth was highly traumatic, leaving me with pain, confusion, a deep need for repair, and love for my bonding with my firstborn son. The second birth was magical and trauma-free, but not without pregnancy anxieties to manage. There was tons of emotional processing to do in order to not bring into the birth space the wounds and fears of the past. The emotional and spiritual pre-birth communication connections with my babies gave us another layer of healing. This helped as we moved forward, acknowledged our power, and got empowered toward raising a family.

Labor and birthing are not the same for everyone, and that is a valuable thing to remember and claim. This is definitely a personal experience, and it is meant to be a natural experience of how the mammalian ways of our species thrive so humanity can survive. The birth space requests a certain natural instinct, just like spirit baby communication. The private and natural space of how birth unfolds with our children must be held to a high and respectful regard, with as little intervention as possible, in my opinion. I believe that it does not deserve intervening unless absolutely necessary. Before you go crazy over this, remember that the maternity system has created too much intervention and fear, and be sure to educate yourself and learn about your instinctual nature of motherhood to make choices and decisions.

Your Labor Is a Relationship of Energy for You and Baby

Later, I will take you on a journey of how we are subconsciously connected to the way we give birth through our own personal traumas and lineage. But, first, I want to take you into the magic and love of birthing life.

Human life is born through the body, and that alone is the most extraordinary miracle. You enter into labor, and your body prepares for a physiological birth for your child and you. The beautiful synergistic connection of mother's body and baby's body takes place within a deep knowing. That knowing is highly intelligent. It holds its own distinct information like a code that is encoded into the cells. The design is by nature, and it is guided by natural instincts to follow and more to develop.

Pre-birth communication can support labor as it is a natural part of birthing. As labor is initiated, that natural oxytocin high and uninterrupted hormones do what they are meant to do and support contractions or some call waves of labor. The body of mother and baby prepares and the fluids and muscles working with energy to keep it moving and on a chemical and physical level that includes a spiritual level, all to enter the world. Moving into the wisdom of connection and communication with baby and body is all you really need. Ideally, any support outside of you watches the miracle of life with power and love and only engages when truly necessary and not sooner or later. Pre-birth communication will give so much to the labor and birthing space.

When you start your pre-birth communication in any trimester of your pregnancy, you are giving to that spiritual parenting relationship before birth. Basically, you are saying that your child is real, and exists, and your energy of love and connection expands with intuition. You and baby are mutually in and out of a psychic plane of consciousness and existence together to communicate without anything else, but that.

The power of pre-birth communication during labor, especially during early labor, will continue to give to how you both connect on a most deep and present level into life. It allows space to be who you are and who you are allowing yourself to be with less fear and less mental tension or distraction. As we know, the mind constricts often with fear, and that creates an obstacle or block when natural physiological birth wants to unfold and happen on its own terms with little to no obstructions. This is why childbirth education can be positive if properly taught by someone you resonate with, or it can be self-acquired through your own self-education. There's no wrong way to do it. Another supportive tool that is a great collaboration with pre-birth communication is hypnosis before or during birth. Other complementary holistic tools to add include acupuncture, cranial sacral, body massage, energy healing like Reiki or touch therapy, and more. Holistic modalities can create a balance of space, an ease to let go, and an opening in the birth space so mother and baby can do what they know how to do.

Waking Up to Healing Emergencies or Interventions – Don't Be Scared

Most birthing inconsistencies are connected to energy and the lifestyle of the mother. The external environment can easily reflect the internal environment unconsciously. Stress is a huge part of pregnancy into birth. It is normal. Stress has its purpose, but too much anxiety, as we know, is not very encouraging for overall health, even generally. Unfortunately, in our cultures of developed societies with overstimulation, electromagnetic fields to battle, and other toxicities, health and birthing are made more challenging. At times, there will be birth challenges, such as the baby being in a different position, a heart rate change, and other issues. But it seems today that many birth outcomes are lined up as an instant emergency, and mothers are set up for that due to the policies, procedures, and care models implemented. I may look at this in more depth in another conversation or book on coming back to nature and mother intuition and baby.

I am noticing that hospital births are notorious for high intervention. I have not heard of any hospital setting not intervening in small or big ways. It is a problem that many are working on to change as birth workers, advocates, and change-makers keep implementing better ways for mothers and babies.

Whatever your birth options are, be in deep intuitive awareness with it. Check in with yourself and check in with your baby. Remember, your pregnancy and birth are not a problem to be fixed or tampered with. The extremeness of interventions can become way too much for mothers and babies. This can leave mother and baby feeling unattached, not bonded, exhausted emotionally, and more. Repair and restructuring will be necessary, which can take days to months to a lifetime. The birth imprint stays with each of us in this lifetime. The Birth Psychology field goes deeper into this healing and wellness in the most extraordinary ways of science and psychology.

The organization that explores and studies this is one to follow – **the Association of Prenatal and Perinatal Psychology and Health (APPPAH). www.birthpsychology.com**

The truth is nobody wants trauma, but, of course, it happens. Trauma is so impactful and healing is evident hopefully after. We are set up to thrive and survive. Babies hold all their memory and information in their nervous system, as they are developing. That means we humans, as an embryo, are a neural tube first to later become the spine, brain, and more. The existence of the neural tube means that your baby is already taking in information from the very moments of cellular creation. That is incredible... isn't it!? The memories begin inside the womb of the mother before life, and later the brain and mind can translate and interpret through body and mind communication. Even though the biology of the body is transcribing energetic information, it is precious to know that the spirit of the baby already knows and communicates nevertheless.

I am passionate about women, pregnancy, birth, and babies and I am going to get your energy excited or pissed off by what I am saying next. Birth has been hijacked and the takeover has been going on way too long. You are ready to take responsibility and create an easy, gentle, and loving birth. *Birthing Without Violence* by Federick Leboyer, M.D. revolutionized how we view infants' own experiences of birth. He is one of many who have changed how birthing, the infant, and the mother are treated and supported. No longer are the days when most women come freely into their natural connection of birth with their bodies and babies, but I have hope for it with many having home births and unassisted births. I want this statement to poke and trigger you into thinking about how and where you will be giving birth. I hate to say it, but often a fight for a physiological birth is occurring. I do not say that to discourage you; I say that because I want you to wake up, listen, and bring your baby into a safe environment so the future is protected. You are ready and pre-birth communication will keep guiding you through the next steps into birthing, mothering, and/or fathering your newborn into life.

The experience of birth is a choice, but sometimes things get switched up and the energies of the past create an undesirable experience. The consciousness of birth seeped throughout history has really created a very strong imprint that birth is dangerous, and so it gets given over to another authority that is not you. The false ideas that I want you to break free from will hold birth in a way that needs changing. Birth is not dangerous, but it can be when intervened and over-medicalized. So know that death is a part of birth with or without intervention, no matter what. It is something that will always live in mystery, at least for now.

What about cesarean births and pre-birth communication?

Cesarean births are also known as "C-sections" or "surgical births." I naively wrote many years ago a 15-page manual called *Sacred Cesarean Birth*. It was a guide for a sacred entrance into the world and for raising awareness by following a kind philosophy within cesarean birth. I wrote this mostly because of my own birth into the world as I was born by a non-labored cesarean breech. I felt that we can improve birth with awareness for mothers to take action in their cesarean births through information, but mostly intuition. Intuition has a way of healing, and it offers less trauma or rapid healing of trauma within a more mindful approach to cesarean through family-centered cesarean, kind cesarean, gentle c-section, and natural cesarean.

I do not want to pretend that cesarean births are beneficial just because a compassionate cesarean is built. Cesarean births are not without risk. It has been heard from the mouths of mothers to be a very traumatic experience. Not just mother, but baby also. It is serious with complications at times. I understand that mothers are very strong-willed, very strong-bodied, and very strong-minded. Regardless, a cesarean birth leaves a very huge birthing imprint. This will impact not just the mother's experience in her body and mind, but also the birth of her child imprinted into this world and together their connection with this world. Again, I say this not to create more fear, but within the power of prevention and energy of self-awareness and embodiment.

I have to add that there is a saying I have heard for many years that those born through cesarean have a more psychic expansive awareness. Meaning, a more psychic connection comes because that early foundation of being born traumatically creates a rift in consciousness. In return comes an energetic awareness of other worlds. I am not sure why, but I can imagine more about it, whether true or not.

I want to share the healing for you in this. A cesarean birth happens, and you can over-analyze it after, but work hard not to do so. A deeper healing is needed, and over time you will make peace with it. But in the early days afterward, you will be in repair. I had a vision not too long ago that children that are to be born by cesarean come as a sacrifice to heal deeper wounds. I was surprised by this insight because I often wondered why this is such an intense birth for so many. Our children are sacrificing themselves. It goes deeper into changing and creating new energy that is very individual.

Not all cesarean births will be the same, and not all souls, bodies, and mothers will have the same experience. I do believe we have a choice in how we want to birth, but you can see what happens. I am not writing this to shame, trigger, or blame you, but I do feel as if birthing mothers need to be free from victimization. Nobody signs up and says they want a traumatic birth. But the history of the mother and then connected to her own family lineage and or past lives is often where it originates from. Sometimes it feels like this can be preventable and maybe it can be, but it takes a certain frequency from mother and baby. Something that needs exploring and discovering.

I am not anti-medicine or anti-doctor. I am pro people knowing themselves to make choices and remembering the nature of body and mind intelligence. It is really important if you are giving birth in a hospital to make sure to know the cesarean birth rates and the rates from the doctor and the staff and what their view is on cesarean births. Do not be afraid to share your birth plan with your hospital if you are leaning towards that kind of birth, or for backup and creating a checklist if a cesarean birth happens. Remember, in birth, your baby is in deep-heart communication with you every step of the way, and your job is to listen and be alert to healing. You can communicate with your baby intuitively and psychically before the cesarean birth and even after on a spiritual level. Keep being in pre-birth communication practice to continue with it into the life of the newborn and the healing forward that wants to come.

What about hospital births, center births, home births, and unassisted births?

What does your spirit baby say or feel about it?

You won't hear babies asking for difficult outcomes. I believe that is an Earth problem coming from the energy of societies and more. Where you give birth is where you feel the most comfortable, open, and available. It has to be from an expanded energetic aware place. I do feel like hospital births are going to become more obsolete as we evolve on our deepest levels. I imagine taking back power to shift into safer births through birthing centers or at home with midwives and birth attendants, but also birthing unassisted/free births. We are really in a time of bringing back our autonomy to our own bodies, with wisdom and healing that comes from us.

In order for you to own your connection with your baby, you must actually take action to make your life different and listen with deep levels of intuition to clear the body and get the nervous system regulated to allow room for experiencing. Becoming a parent is about raising your own vibrational self and listening to your spirit baby in your conception, in pregnancy, and into parenthood.

You own your pregnancy and birth, and it can only be taken away by fear. Keep your heart free and connected with your baby. Do your research on how and where you can birth best. Get a doula or join a birth education group to protect and guide you to believe in yourself and stay connected with your baby. Know your rights and know what consent means. I leave your birth journey up to you and nobody else. Trust that you will keep learning, creating, and healing.

What about twin babies and spirit baby communication?

On this subject, I want to share some curious thoughts and insights...

Two sweet girls of the same age are holding hands next to each other. They are playing in the space. Then she is dancing with her sister, who is her twin. They want to come and be born, but they are not sure how, when, or if they will be coming together. "I like dolphins," the sweet girl says. "And my sister likes yellow flowers." They share information about who they are and how they are connected with their mother.

Twins are very unique, in my perspective. Multiple births offer a special connection, and twins come to families who are ready for it. Some feel like they can invite twins in and do life differently in order to have twins. I don't know for sure if eating certain foods or following calendars will increase the chances of twins. The spirit baby messages and energies shared are to support and heal the dynamics of life with this experience of twins and/or triplets.

In the psychic space with twins, I have experienced conception-potential twins and pregnancy twins. Honestly, it's like a big old party offering conversation with different Soul Personalities and energies shared with mother and/or father. Twins will come to those, as I say, that are ready to experience that specific dynamic.

I have worked with many kinds of twin energies – some being both girls, some both boys, and others a girl and a boy. What I've noticed about twin spirit babies is sometimes they want to come together and other times years apart as siblings. But, in any case, a psycho-spiritual twin connection will remain forever. That means, they have a special agreement and bond that is witnessed earthside and they both feel it and know it.

In sessions of spirit baby readings, where I have communicated with twins...

Twins through IVF, naturally conceived twins, and I have heard of twin siblings or twiblings

- I have seen twins in conception into pregnancy through IVF where a mother-to-be knew where her son and her daughter were located inside her womb and she was correct. Her sense was confirmed at the cesarean birth.

- I have seen twins in pregnancy through natural conception, that had things to share about who they were and how to support them.

- I have seen twins that were miscarried, unfortunately – there were many sessions related to this loss.

- I have seen twins that were stillborn, unfortunately – there were many sessions related to this loss.

- I have seen twins where one twin survives and the other twin dies in utero or after being born.

Twin-ergy and the Magic of Spirit Baby Communication

Spirit baby communication with twins is no different than singletons. IVF, natural twin conception, or twiblings (see definition below). The hardest part of twin spirit baby or pre-birth communication is learning how to tune into the psychic energy of each child. I often notice in earthside children, as well as in conception and pregnancy, that there is always a twin that may not seem as strong as the other one. Both physically and psychically, I do believe that there is some kind of scientific explanation for that symbiotic shared relationship, whether they are identical or fraternal. It takes a lot of energy and development to grow.

If you are trying to conceive – maybe you're going through IVF or you're naturally conceiving – you may or may not know the outcomes. Keep talking to your two different babies' souls. Even outside of twins with just siblings, quite often there are more than one spirit baby. I've seen this many times with mothers and fathers. If you are in pre-birth communication with your twins, then keep communicating and connecting with your babies.

I once met a friend of a friend who used the word "twiblings." It was new to my awareness. Twiblings is when two genetically related babies are born from a mother and gestational carrier or surrogate or two different surrogates. The friend was trying to conceive and decided to get an embryo from her and her husband for a surrogate. She became pregnant not too soon after her surrogate became pregnant. She thought of them as a type of twin.

I want to share a transcript from *Spirit Baby Radio* about twins. One of the things I share is how to create an altar and a space where you can work to call in your twin energy. Then you have to surrender and see what unfolds.

Transcript from *SPIRIT BABY RADIO* – About Twins!

Stories & ways to call in twins & more

> *Welcome to Episode 66. An invitation of twins – siblings being born together. How do you welcome multiples into your life? What kind of pregnancy is it? What does it mean when siblings want to be born together? What's the difference between IVF twins and natural twins?*
>
> *And how does the spirit baby world work with twins? It's very unique to you. It's not like it works one way or another. I've seen twins, many twins. Sometimes they want to be born apart and sometimes they come together. Sometimes it's hard to share that information, to know the truth of it. And with one woman, we talked to a boy and a girl for a long time. She did conceive twins, but they didn't make it and she had a miscarriage. And then the twins, the boy and a girl, they actually came separately within a year or two apart, which was very fascinating. This woman was very committed to her twinergy and connecting with these baby beings, because she felt it.*

And I had a friend who had a miscarriage and she was so devastated. It was really hard, she had to grieve. And then after that, she became pregnant with twins naturally, which was such a shock. But I thought that was interesting because it's like the baby, one was coming, but then was like "Wait a minute. Nope, I need to come with my sister." And so the boy and girl needed to be born together.

And what does that mean to have a twin altar? A twin altar has everything of twos in it. Two goddesses, two babies, two flowers, two crystals. It is how you want to create that altar. Two things of baby stuff, maybe you feel two boys, maybe you feel two girls, maybe you feel a boy and a girl. Put an altar in your little corner space, in a little window sill, and even a little box somewhere. Wherever it is, talk to those baby energies. Invite them in; create a meditation around it.

How do you open to twin energy and how do you allow that to move through you? Visualize that you are receiving through your right hand, and your left hand, as though you're holding them out. That you're receiving and pulling that energy down into your womb space from your right hand down, left hand down, into your womb space. And breathe with that and say, "I'm here to be a host to these beings that I feel are connecting and communicating with me."

Since I mentioned twiblings, I wanted to add that I will not go into deeper details into surrogacy – even though I have had sessions with spirit babies for parents with surrogates, while meeting the mother that was not carrying the child. If this is you, then I want to encourage spirit baby communication as the mother borrowing a womb temporarily with your own embryo or adopted embryo(s). I urge you to connect for you and your baby. Motherhood comes in many ways and this counts. And so do your spiritual connections.

CHAPTER NINE

Miscarriage – The Afterlife of Spirit Baby - 1

"You are a child of the Universe

A soul star of the night sky

So love yourself as you are

Sacred Creatress of Cosmic love "

~ **Madeline K Adams, Soul Star Child of the Universe**

She was a fun and fiery spirit, but not ready to come. Her brother, who was calm and joyful in his spirit, would be next. But then something changed, and he was not ready yet. This mother is experiencing her multiple losses, which have left her with sadness, heart disappointment, and uncertainty. Her spirit children want her to understand that alignment is coming and a depth of healing would soon be guiding her.

I will never minimize the deep heartache and profound transformation of healing that occurs through:

- early loss of miscarriage,
- later loss of stillbirth,
- infancy loss after life,

- sudden infant death syndrome (SIDS), and
- children that die days, weeks, to months after being born.

I hear you and I am listening.

Miscarriage is more common than many realize, and it is an early gestational loss up to 20 weeks. I want you to know that every pregnancy counts. Miscarriage birth can easily be dismissed because it is an early loss, but that does not mean it hurts less or that you should be treated with less love and kindness. It affects young women and older women of all races around the world because it does not judge.

The kinds of miscarriage are:

- complete,
- ectopic,
- chemical,
- blighted ovum, and/or
- silent miscarriage.

All matter, whether single or multiple losses. It is suggested that genetic issues, health, toxicities, stress, and environmental pollutants can bring the results of a spontaneous loss like this. The shocking and sudden news that your pregnancy did not continue deserves love, compassion, and space to grieve.

Birth loss came to me not by my own experience, but by women showing up needing healing and deeply held support so they can bring their babies earthside and honor the ones that will not. Loss belongs to the mysterious, which often can be a cruel experience for mothers and fathers. The spirit of these babies is more than just in-between worlds to be lost or forgotten. Babies in spirit are fully alive and doing well, if not coming back to Earth at a different time, gender, or through the family in the future. These souls or spirits exist and communicate through the fields of energy around your own consciousness in many ways, such as thought forms, feelings, sensations, and knowings.

I have witnessed spirit babies within miscarriage in private sessions have big things to share. I am going to go more into how to use spirit baby communication, specifically through miscarriage, in ways that can offer you the deepest healing beyond anything I've ever seen within loss.

Spirit Baby Communication & Miscarriage

I want to encourage you to speak to your baby between the compassionate loving spaces of your own heart's healing. Even if you feel like you're not receiving any specific communication, just acknowledge that there is something happening. Over the days, you will move into deep ceremonial spaces of healing. You'll be in a sacred connection to your body and speaking to your child in the spiritual realms so that you can heal and receive what is next. I recommend that you sit with yourself and call upon the space to be filled with tenderness and self-love. That may be your hardest perspective to achieve, but also the most needed and a priority.

What does spirit baby say about your miscarriage?

Your experience is your own, which means how you feel and experience your loss is important. In this healing, you will find answers and get into a deeper relationship with yourself. Do not waste your time being difficult with judgment and denial, shame, or guilt. You are the one who needs to open up to your intuitive heart so your clarity and grounding insights can be revealed.

You have to understand that your baby and/or babies have messages for you. You do have a baby and they are here now in spirit form. Miscarriage can be seen as a passage. The birth of life, just like death, is a passageway that everyone must be with and wake up to undergoing. Your experience of loss will not be linear, and you will feel major changes that will impact you forever because it is meant to do so. Together you and baby will discover and create a new energy and belief that will most definitely heal everyone involved deeply.

Did I do something wrong?

Why did my baby leave?

What does my spirit baby need to be born?

First, I want you to know you did nothing wrong. The loss has many layers and elements as to the why, how, and what to do next. It is a very common experience to question what went wrong. I do believe that this is something you're meant to explore. You may not get the answers that you want, and you may be pushed into more or less scientific advice or evidence. However, oftentimes you may end up with no answers. I do feel that the answers are always spiritual in nature, especially within miscarriage. So be aware of fighting the mind over the heart. Let the heart guide you.

I have had many spirit babies share that the genetic vessel was not healthy enough for them to enter and/or something more for the parents needs to be spiritually explored for the mother and/or father to heal. I have listened to mothers share that their babies' cords were pinched, there were genetic anomalies, or placental issues could be the reason. When that biological and medical support is given as a possible reason, then the mother and/or father can feel a tiny sense of peace. But then what happens next is the over-questioning and wondering if they, as the parents, could have prevented it, should have known better, or could figure out whose fault it is. This is because it's human nature to fault, to get the right answers, and to use science to understand situations. However, in truth, there are great mystical mysteries that will never align with science. Outside science, another quantum awareness lives in a miraculous and curious place. It is where a deeper intuitive journey begins and a new territory of self-discovery is being asked of you. I know you can do it and you will do it because you are ready for this.

This is why I believe that science can never truly figure it out; but like any good scientist with thought-provoking theories, they should keep trying as humanity continues to evolve in so many ways for our future. When we can come into more spiritual openness and awareness, then the energetic principles of spirit and body will come into our minds like known information. The answers we crave so much about conception and miscarriage are not inside the mind of the brain to figure it out, but exist in another part of your own spirit. It is a sensing and visceral place, and that is the language there. It is experiential, kinesthetic, and craves presence. It is of our own frequency. Frequency meaning, it is you inside your physical body and beyond this world and into who you truly are as an electromagnetic force and light, we can say. Everyone is a frequency. It is within everyone to have energetic knowledge, and it is time to remember and connect with it as easily as the breath and the way one touches life.

Spirit baby does have a message for you in your experience. It is not to prove anything to you or show you fear and suffering. It is the opposite. Your message will be shared with you as long as you are open to it. It can remain with much sorrow or unknowns, but transformation is here. You must go into a quiet and deep place and find your inward connection to yourself. Be with the grief and be with the changing energy behind it. Then you get led by what comes next.

After a miscarriage – whether you've experienced medical support or you've naturally birthed on your own or with other support – the most important thing to do is to be with your emotions and your grief. You must recognize your loss, and you must go inward into the sacred spaces of healing. That may mean having shock, denial, anger, and weepiness. I will say it again – you have to be with your very own grief. Remember that the grief is going to make you question everything, tell you to have a plan, try to move you away from your grief and jump out of it, instead of being inside with it. It is very important to connect with your emotional and psychological well-being and know what kind of support you need –whether that is counseling, therapies, or other healing medical support.

After a miscarriage, take time to be tender, have self-compassion, and practice extreme self-care for yourself. The healing is physical, emotional, mental, and spiritual. Allow your body to rebuild on a cellular, blood, and energetic level to come back into a cycle so it can restructure and repair. When you are in spiritual healing, then you can connect with your spirit baby.

Why can't I hear or sense my baby after the miscarriage?

It is normal to feel like your baby has left you or that something is wrong because maybe you don't feel that connection as you did during pregnancy. I want to make sure that you understand what's happening, and let's label that as grief because it is. I promise that your baby has not left you for something or someone else. Know that the grief will keep you in certain spaces that include fear and intense processing and releasing.

It is very common after miscarriage to feel like you're not connecting with your spirit baby anymore. Yet I have not once ever seen spirit babies leave their parents after miscarriage and have no communication at all. Actually, spirit babies are so loving and present with their mothers and fathers.

Spirit babies are full of love, joy, exuberance, and light. They never have anything negative to say about their parents; in the energy of the spirit baby space (which we can call a dimension), there is no such thing as negativity. Negativity only exists as an earthly concept, and it is an experience they do not need or understand. They can, at times, try to translate messages that you might perceive as negative, and that's something to keep in mind.

The biggest challenge in receiving your connection with spirit baby communication is all the information available within the New Age and/or spiritual communities. Everyone is going to have different experiences, and that feels important to remember. Many of these ideas can be psychic experiences, dreams, and interpretations around miscarriage specifically.

I want you to pause and receive yourself. Some see miscarried babies who go to Heaven or the afterlife as never coming back or getting reborn within reincarnation. I cannot confirm nor deny any one of those ideas 100% for everyone because different stories for different soul healings exist. Some miscarried babies come back to Earth and others will not. Some may ask where do they go if they do not come back to Earth? Some do not need to be born or have already experienced what they need. Others will come back to other family members and or other families some say, other lifetimes upon Earth, or other galactic lifetimes. I will never promise a definitive answer for your own journey. Be open to your healing with your spirit baby communication relationship and see what comes to you. I encourage you, after having any loss, to not give up on your spirit baby. Don't give up on your spirit baby communication practices.

Remember that it is okay to question your baby and why they are not here with you, despite how much they are loved and wanted. I can promise you as fact that everything that you communicate to your baby – whether it's through your mind, heart, feelings, or energy – your spirit baby hears and receives. I connect with thousands of babies, and they want their parents to know that they are real, the parents are being heard, and your messages are received. And that they are connecting with you, not just by love but through your own soul and energy.

Why isn't my baby ready to be born? How do you welcome your baby back after miscarriage?

I am going to share what I shared in the fertility chapter because this could be similar with birth loss in why the baby was not born:

- The current timeline of your life is active with unresolved trauma.

- The issues are connected to <u>your specific</u> childhood/lineage/ancestral trauma and past.
- The issues are connected to <u>your partner's</u> childhood/lineage/ancestral trauma and past.
- The issues are a <u>past life</u> that is active in the current timeline of healing.
- The issues are <u>spiritual</u>: involving multidimensional/galactic realms/other realities.
- The issues are connected to the <u>spirit of your child</u>: related to the above list.

How do you open up to spirit baby after a single or multiple loss?

You welcome your baby or babies back because you know it is your path. You do the healing work. You do it because you are strong, even with fragile edges. You are a creator and you are worthy of it. Basically, you just do it!

The next time you become pregnant, I know you will feel scared and unsure, and that is all okay. You have permission to feel and experience loss in any way that you need to do so. Remember that each pregnancy is different, whether earthborn or not. You keep communicating and listen, heal, and follow what is the next step forward.

5 Tips for Working with Spirit Baby Communication Post-Miscarriage

1. Tend to your heart and be self-compassionate. Focus on yourself first and go inward with your breath and body.

2. Sit in the quiet and light a candle. Breathe and meditate together with you and your spirit baby.

3. Speak to your spirit baby from your heart, feeling and touching your heart and womb-belly space.

4. Share your dreams with your spirit baby, like you are having a conversation with your baby that sits with you.

5. Let signs, symbols, thoughts, and messages come through to you. Just receive it.

Medical issues, sicknesses, and disabilities...

My medical disclaimer is that I cannot diagnose or confirm whether the health of one's baby is meant to be a certain way or not. Though something I am not going to go into deeply, I want to bring a little bit of energy to the children who are born sick, or with medical issues and disabilities. I want to begin by saying that the soul is perfect. That the created body can come into sickness or disabilities. The reason is very unique to the family history/lineage, genetic energetic storylines, and healing lessons. I am sorry if this challenges you, and I know a life is never without a purpose. Spirit baby has something to share in this lifetime together with you, and they have a path to follow as well.

Many years ago, I personally supported women who had babies and shared that the children had different medical anomalies or issues. I do feel like it's a very fragile conversation that I no longer will talk about or offer readings with. Medical intervention can easily make mistakes and create unneeded stress, and other times it offers very grounding, supportive information.

Many children will be born disabled and have other diagnoses. I do not share this information with mothers and fathers and there's a reason why. I do not want to be available for it and I do not feel it serves a purpose. That agreement is between a parent and a child on a deep spiritual level. I will not interfere with it. There's nothing wrong with a child who is born sick or disabled and has a mission that you may not understand until you are in it. I hold pure love and trust that the mission is powerful, healing, and full of love.

Do not fear that something is wrong with your baby unless it is. This is why spirit baby communication can bring you so much support and self-awareness by listening and making choices to best give to you and your baby. Some children may not share with you that they are coming into a challenging body or it may not be in your best interest to know. Another reason is parents do not want to believe it.

Error can happen and so does denial. Sometimes medical scans and tests do not pick up something that is off with development, and other times it can be very clear and unmistakable. It is very hard for a parent to be in a not-knowing place about what the world will bring to a child who is not healthy or will have daily challenges for the rest of life. The best advice that I can give is for you to read through the chapters and get very strong on your trusting intuition and psychic styles. For you to be able to dismantle old parts of your stories in life and recreate a new consciousness by your own heart's wisdom. By this I mean, connect with yourself first, and allow your child to connect with you in this special journey of difficulty and needed healing. You are allowed to ask your child to come into a healthy body and mind. After that, you have to let go and see what unfolds.

It is your choice to find peace and solace in your spirit baby exploration practices. Remember that you are unique in your connection and how you are showing up for it. Keep moving into healthy and full-term pregnancy intentions, energy/frequency, and mindset. Your child has a purpose and you will discover it along the way. I hold you in ease and an infinite amount of love and compassion for the experience that you are going through. I am trusting that the energy here will bring you some sense of self-trust and interconnectedness. I hold that your heart keeps leading you and that your baby ushers you forward into a life of beauty and renewal.

Surrogacy/Gestational Carrier, and Adoption

I want to note that I am not going to expand on these topics of conception into birth, and I will only share this small section of it. It has been a limited area I have worked with, but feels very valuable to add and give some energy to what I can share and have supported.

Spirit baby communication offers so much if you are doing surrogacy/gestational carrier, or adoption. Spirit baby communication works even when you are a parent receiving your child through another body. You can definitely build a spirit baby communication practice through the guidance in this book. I have personally worked with women who have gone through surrogacy and typically for severe medical issues or challenging infertility. Babies in spirit will and do share messages in cases I have taken within surrogacy and adoption. I've discovered that there can be a lineage and past-lives issues involved in this outcome to parenthood. To clarify lineage, it is one's ancestry. It is the roots of the past from families that through the generations have an influence, and I share this because it has an effect on the present time, whether it is conscious or unconscious. Most people tend to have unconscious material that comes to the surface in different ways. Spirit baby so-called "agreements" can go back before you even considered pregnancy and parenthood. It is a very curious inquiry and place to explore. So if you or somebody you know is going into surrogacy or adoption, please review the early chapter on conception and pregnancy with spirit baby communication, and let this guide you because it can greatly.

I am only going to share a little bit of two related stories, and out of privacy, I will change the names and share insights specific to surrogacy with spirit baby communication.

A mother came to me looking to have a second child and was experiencing multiple miscarriages and unknown infertility status. I am going to call her Sasha. Sasha was a wonderful woman and already had a lovely daughter. In our session together, it was discovered that Sasha had a past-life connection with the surrogate and her son. I found it fascinating that Sasha actually went to the country to have a vacation that I named. The past-life of herself, her surrogate, and her son took place in that country. It was such an incredible session because this particular country is not a common country, and there was something deeper in the story of this particular surrogate that I was able to articulate and share. I do not think this could have happened and would have been so profound without Sasha being open and receptive of how her son was ready to come into life with them.

Adoption and Spirit Baby Communication

I definitely do not want to leave out adoption, but I don't have much to share when it comes to the adoption of babies and children already earthside. What I can share from the private session space is that the field of energy holds a specific vibration for adoption. How I have seen adoption in the auric/energy field is when somebody is open to it or actually taking action to do it. That energy needs to integrate, and it can bring in a loving kind of family agreement. This takes opening and sitting in a receptive state for it. For your potential adoption of a child, what I've seen is that children are happy and welcoming about coming through this way. The path for the children and the family adopting them is about healing lineage and creating a new life together. I have often seen adopted children, after many years in the family, look like their biological families, even though no genetic makeup is shared. I think that is so awesome, and it shows how our environment is very powerful and how our body restructures and reshapes based on life experiences.

Spirit baby communication works beautifully with adoption, especially if your heart is bonded with it before and the rest comes together through energy first and later through legalities and institutes. Knowing that you're receiving through this sacred way will teach and guide you. Following the spirit baby communication information in the conception and the pregnancy chapters will support you in adoption. Remember that psychic awareness can and will build your heart-to-heart communication and connection. It is up to you to do it.

I am going to share another story. With it, I'm going to give you a little insight into adoption with spirit baby communication. I have personally worked with women who, though not specifically coming for spirit-baby adoption readings, were open to adoption and gave that energy outward for it, while holding hope for their own child. It is normal and okay to have both dreams and desires.

Sometimes both are the outcome and not uncommon, like in the twiblings information discussed earlier.

I will name her Sophie. She was a single, strong woman who had a heart of gold. She wanted a child in her life and opened up to any way that would come. Her IVF conception did not work out, leaving her with a later loss. She was very open to adoption, but was on a list, and it felt like this would never happen. We worked together in sessions to open up the lines of energy between her heart and her spirit babies. To the surprise of us all, she received not only one invitation to foster, but another months later. Both fosters involved boys and her loss was a boy. Her foster son became an adoption and her son Kyle would be in her life. Kyle was a light and joyful being, and it happened because she was in the energy of it. She was opening her field of mothering, the birth of this being came through in another way, and she received him.

I find something extremely fascinating; it is quite often said that many women on a long journey of conception will explore adoption, and then immediately after the adopted child arrives, the woman gets pregnant. Nobody can say for sure whether after adoption and/or even surrogacy that the mother will become pregnant herself. Some would say love hormones are working harder, and biology and the environment take over. Others would believe it was meant to be by spirit and God, and that the baby was waiting for her or his sibling to come through adoption.

Awakening to Your Wholeness - Let Your Spirit Guide You

Coming back to early loss. Know that your miscarriage is now a part of your life and will leave a memory. It is your own pregnancy and birth cut short. It is a journey and an experience you get to alchemize into love and personal evolution. You have to accept that you somehow embodied death inward, and there's something sacred and somber about that. I will keep encouraging you to receive your heart's messages and receive the support that you deserve. Take all the lost parts and hold them together so they find each other. Remember that you are due for loving tender interconnection. Sometimes you have to hit hard places in the shadows to step upward into softness and light. I love you and I hold you in the deepest regard. Your child or children love you too.

PRACTICES WITH SPIRIT BABY COMMUNICATION

Love Practice of Communication – Miscarriage Meditation

- Find a quiet space and sit comfortably.

- Close your eyes, align your spine, and feel your whole body.

- Starting at the top of your head, you'll be moving your awareness slowly down. Check in with yourself first by saying hello to your head and neck. Farther down, say hello to your upper mid-body (chest), then to your breath and lungs, and onto your belly.

- Keep going downward into your lower back and hips saying hello. Then to your legs and feet.

- Let your body's check-in create an open space of ease and relaxation.

- Next, bring your attention to your heart and listen to your spiritual heart center.

- You are ready to invite your spirit baby into the space of your heart.

- Share a personal love statement from your heart and let this example guide you: *Hello my baby being, I am here for you. I miss you. I am open to understanding our relationship. I am ready. I love you.*

- I want you to receive as you are placing your hands in your heart space and letting a spiral of light and the essence of your spirit baby being inward. In the spiral of light you are receiving and you are giving. You are in connection with your child.

- Begin to sense, feel, know, and visualize what it is that you need now and how you can continue to prepare your mind, heart, and your womb.

- Sit with your breath and let trust and know you are being heard and received.

- When you feel complete after 10 to 20 minutes, then end your meditation with prayer or an intention of gratitude and love.

Notes From a Spirit Baby Medium

MEDITATION - AUDIO Version

Direct Link:
https://www.newearthchildren.com/meditationnotes-from-spiritbaby

QR Code:

CHAPTER TEN

Still Birth/Infancy Death – The Afterlife of Spirit Baby - 2

"Imagine what this grieving space does for an individual facing loss. It grants profound permission to enter a place of sorrow, to work with it, to explore its contours and textures, to become familiar with the landscape of loss."

*~ Frances Weller, **The Wild Edge of Sorrow: Rituals of Renewal and the Sacred Work of Grief***

A light-child boy shared the most beautiful energy with me for his mother. I feel he wants others to understand and sit with this insight. His mother wanted this to be shared with you.

He left his Earth body at two years old. I will call him Nova. He shares many messages. Nova is a child of light and wants his mother and everyone to know that when your spirit child sends you a message of a living creature – like animals, insects, or other – it is not a random sign, but more of a message of Life. That your child is creating a way to feel her or his energy through that life force. In our world, we easily connect with a living force that embodies spirit. So when you see that creature, please understand your child is affecting its cellular body and conscious spirit in order to touch you with the energy of life, remembrance, and healing.

It is time to awaken more to your infinite self. So when an animal or insect comes into your life, be open to feeling, receiving, sensing, and trusting the wise message(s). Your child of light communicates with you probably more than you may recognize. Open up your empathic channels, accept your psychic self, and use your telepathic energies. They exist, and it is a serious path of truth, love, and Spirit.

Forever a Baby - Spiritual Communication

Stillbirth happens to 1% of all pregnancies. A stillbirth is a later pregnancy loss that occurs between 20 to 40 weeks. It is common for a baby who is doing great with no problems to then have no heartbeat. Just like a miscarriage, stillbirths happen within all races of women, all around the world, and for many different reasons. Some reasons include, but are not limited to:

- maternal risk to infections
- hemorrhages, and
- placental abruptions.

Perhaps none of those fit your own experience of a stillbirth.

I know you probably have so many questions that may never receive the right answers or an answer that will satisfy your heart's love and desire to have your son or daughter earthside in your life. It is a true tragedy that mothers and fathers have to experience losing a child. If you have experienced a stillbirth, then your heart is understandably deeply impacted, and the healing called forth will not be with simple instructions. Hopefully, I can provide a change that is enough to get you to where your healing needs you to move towards with ease and support.

I understand that nothing is validating enough to accept the death of your child or children. Your life will be forever altered. The irreparable knowledge of death as a part of your life should be received with respect always. Having the tragic loss of your daughter or son not in your life and only through dreams and psychic energies can offer a salve to the pain. I know it will not change any outcomes, instead how your heart communicates and heals in ways that you never knew possible.

I have had many sessions and workshops supporting stillbirth loss for mothers, fathers, and families. The fear after a stillbirth is a real battle to endure, especially if you are trying to conceive after loss. You will have to learn to assemble new inner workings of self-trust. It is going to be work that is hard. You can and will do it because you have no other choice, and your child of light in spirit is supporting you with it.

Your Heart Bonded With the Soul Of Your Child

Your babies and/or child/children are deeply connected to you, whether with you in pregnancy or birth for weeks to days to years or a lifetime. You have a forever heart contract. That means your child of light is never truly gone. I want you to energize your heart for a moment and take a soft and present breath.

Remember that I came up with the names "children of light" and "child of light," and that is how I will be referring to your spirit child through still birth or infancy loss. Now remember that your child of light is a powerful spirit/soul of energy with personality and power. Your child of light was born from the Universal Light, the stardust of the Cosmos, and/or the source of God. It does not matter what you believe or not believe; what matters is your child is real, and you are in connection. After all, you share something in common, and that is you were also once a spirit baby being and today here to support the next generations with your love.

Be open and drop into the unknown. Your infinite self-love is ready and here. Explore your eternalness as a priority to your self-discovery. Your eternalness is the connection to who you were before this current time. It is the light body and the real you. It lives here now. Explore it with curious endeavor and relax into the insights for self-reflection. You will determine more because your daughter or son is with you and present in spirit-baby communication with you daily, even when you do not realize and even when you do. I am going to teach you and show you more about this.

What happens after a stillbirth and infancy death with a spirit baby and parent(s)?

Many questions during grief and mourning come up in the minds and hearts of parents, especially in the early days of still-born loss and when an infant dies. Questioning everything is normal and necessary. Grieving is a ritual of human nature, and it must be honored for this is the way of dealing and healing.

Questions I have been asked over the years...

- *Why did my baby die?*
- *Is my baby okay?*
- *Did I do something wrong?*
- *Did I not love them enough?*
- *Will my baby come back?*
- *Is it some spiritual agreement?*

I do not have all the answers. So many inner questions you may have and I will try my best to offer insights to support you. These come from my many sessions with many mothers and fathers and their children. I have listened and shared many messages and the child's personal experience in-between worlds.

I am aware that the place of the Afterlife is a common term for where we go when we die. Through the studies of Mediumship, Paranormal Psychology, other death studies, as well as spiritual and religious ideas and philosophies, I would say it is best to remain open to your heart's path and see what new and old beliefs want to be infused or released from who you are and who you are becoming.

It is hard to not get all the answers, especially the right ones that you need so badly. I encourage parents to tend to grief in the traumatic onset of losing a child and to begin to explore communication with their child right away. Waiting is not necessary, and spirit-baby communication can minimize pain and help you heal more deeply. Your trust will be the biggest challenge and the most needed aspect. I already know that communication happens right away. The parent and child bond is special and extremely unique. Life never ends with the body as we understand, but that does not make it easier to have a child that you may never meet in body and life. Every stillbirth is not the same for each mother, father, and child. I acknowledge you and I want you to receive that.

My experience with stillbirths is that your baby does live. It may not be in the human cellular body and physically, but they do live in this other reality or dimension. That is, unless they are re-birthed into another new body and experience. Not all babies in stillbirth come back into life, and I know this is very hard to hear or read, but it is true. This is something a mother intuitively can sense, communicate with, and understand on a personal level. This is not just a wish or desire, but a real connection. Stillbirth will always be an interdimensional experience, like any birth loss, with many questions hanging around with continuous unknowns.

Communication with your child of light involves your purest self and heart with many openings to your intuitive mediumistic abilities. You do not have to be trained in any specific mediumship to connect with your child because this skill of mediumship is already a part of you. You were born into communication with the Afterlife, and I'm going to help you access that natural connection that is inside you. So you can heal massive parts of your heart and transform your journey into love. Be proud of your mission as a mother to your daughter or son that lives as light.

I have supported many stillbirth-born babies and their mothers and fathers. The children of light have a very extraordinary energy and mission about them. You may not see it in the early connection of your loss because you're probably not supposed to or your grief feels mind-altering and overwhelming. Don't worry because this will change, and you will be able to connect, feel and sense, and get messages, signs, and dreams. I trust in you.

I have connected with the most incredible energies from these children, and the purpose of their life is very expansive. These children not only leave an imprint in the field of the sacral and womb space of mother and father, but they leave an imprint into the family, friends, and fellow humans. These imprints are through the interaction of just their presence of energy through their body and heart in utero and/or outside born. That means that your child's energy enters into this reality creating electromagnetic waves of light and other healing forces of a quantum shift that is present. A quantum shift is a change of reality, and it has an effect on consciousness.

I will investigate the questions more deeply below and move you into communication that you can trust and feel empowered by. Your child is and wants to speak with you, and it is time for you to listen and stop blocking your psychic and intuitive connections. Remember, it is natural to connect and you are going to do it and experience the healing you need. That communication is available, and your child will initiate you into a wisdom that is between two worlds of energy – the life space and the death space, and how they merge together. It is a very deep undertaking for you. Your loss is unique, just like that of your partner and/or other family members, and that includes siblings.

Why did my baby die?

You may need to know this or you may not need to know this. You may get somewhat wrong answers, right answers that feel correct, and others that are completely wrong and confusing. Most people will go into the science of death because that's what we have been told to do, and that is the belief system we have all come to an agreement with. Yet spiritual insights can be received, and taken into a different part of the experience of your loss. I feel death belongs in nature and the cycles of life, but it is purely spiritual always.

Take another breath. Check into your heart and feel your feet for a moment. Pause. Know you are loved. You are whole. You are not wrong or bad. You are open and you are curious. It is not uncommon that birth loss is connected to a lineage and/or ancestral line, and some would say past lives. Your experience of loss is unique to you, and not every reason is the same for everyone. Each story of life holds different energies. Please be aware and sensitive with yourself, as you travel into new healing terrain.

It can feel like a sacrificial mission from the past, and truly be hard to not find fault. But try to move slowly, listen to what serves you in each moment, and see who you become. This comes down to your perceptions of how you view your life through yourself. You can fear, judge, and blame yourself or your family lines, but it is more than that. You always have the option to not do fear, judgment, and blame. It will be hard to get your mind wrapped around why your child isn't here and to not over-question the deeper spiritual journey. I give you permission to not hurt yourself more and work on releasing your judgment and fears. If you must cater to it, then allow yourself to move out of it and not stay there too long.

You may not feel a connection with your child all the time or at first. You may not get insights instantly or it may not be enough for you. Have you heard of mediumship therapy and/or psychic medium readings? This is a profound way to bring healing to those that feel disconnected or need answers. I often feel like the loss of a child has many layers to it that require an unwinding of so many parts in order to bring you into your own self-awareness and spiritual heart. That means that you may not understand a huge part of this connection and why your child died. It can take weeks to many years or a lifetime to get it, and still be in self-discovery of what it means, the why and what it's about, and how to serve your heart in the best way.

Is my child okay?

Your baby is 100% okay. I cannot convince you of it because it is your own lane to stay in to travel. But I do trust you to receive without too many superstitions or false ideas. Remember your baby is not lost, nor is your baby gone or in a bad place. Your baby isn't here in an Earth body and not because you did something wrong or your partner did. I have never met a child through loss who has negative experiences in the Other Life, and nothing is ever with malice or evil intent. If you are told or feel this, it is important to remember that it is the human mind and thoughts of fear that create illusions of suffering. This often is not on purpose, but because of trauma or generational superstitions and other practices.

Your sweet baby is love, purity, and wholeness. The child is beauty and grace and connected to your energy forever. I have listened to many babies and spirits share that they are with their family members and friends on the other side. That they are guardians with your soul family. So if you feel that your mother or your father, or your grandmother or your grandfather, or an aunt or an uncle, or any other relatives who have passed on are in communication with her or him, then they most likely are on the other side. Your responsibility is to trust and reach out for guidance.

I have had many spirit babies through stillbirth and infant death share how Grandma was with them, and other times Father or Grandfather were helping care for them, we can say. Forever babies are being held, cared for, and loved. So open your heart to your passed-on loved ones and allow them to support you.

Did I do something wrong? Did I not love them enough?

The biggest question that hurts deeply is asking if you were good enough or if you did something wrong and your baby did not want to be born. That is grief. No, you did not do anything wrong. It is hard to understand that you didn't do anything wrong because the human experience says something has ended and now I must fix and repair it. So it must be my fault. Well, you showed up to be of service to this beautiful soul to connect with in the deepest way for them to come. That deserves recognition, love, bravery, and kudos.

Will my child come back?

Many bereaved mothers have often asked if their baby will come back. I cannot confirm nor deny that there is a possibility that some babies will come back into a different gender, into a different body, and sometimes even into a different part of the family or the generations later on in the family. The hardest part is most mothers in deep grief and loss have a wish and desire or assumption that their baby is returning to them when that is not always true. Oftentimes, the baby has completed their life purpose, even if just for weeks to months.

I can recall supporting babies who died through stillbirth and these souls were open to share with me their siblings on many occasions. I often see when there's a child in-between worlds of energy that may or may not come back, that they often send their sibling – whether it's a girl or boy. I also noticed that the child of light helps their sibling(s) and their mother through the pregnancy into birth. I have to say it is quite an extraordinary and beautiful experience that I didn't know was possible. Until siblings presented it.

I deeply encourage mothers and fathers who have lost a child through a stillbirth or infancy death, whether it's the first-born, middle child, or later child, to allow the energy of the sibling(s) and spirit world to connect everyone and to allow the earthside siblings to connect as well. Siblings have a bond that we may not fully understand and I want to encourage that connection.

Is it some spiritual agreement?

I cannot say that I am 100% sure that the connection to your child through loss was a pre-written spiritual agreement. I do understand and believe that we have opportunities or some would call it a kind of death exit option to stay or to leave. I am sure it can be comforting when you have experienced loss to understand that maybe there is a deeper purpose and maybe you're not even really sure what that deeper purpose is. So if you feel like your child's purpose was to spend moments in the womb, then you get to sit in that belief and receive it. I am never going to confirm that or even deny that this is a possibility. Again it is something that brings comfort to some mothers and fathers to know that there was a contract or spiritual agreement. Meanwhile, others may feel it is false, and no predestined contractor agreement would ever be that intense and one has possibilities and freedom of choice.

You will come to receive and somehow partially accept that you have been called into the Bereavements Moms Club with a forever membership. Some would call it an initiation into something you would have never chosen. It is hard to understand, resolve, and figure out. I want you to not try, push, or force anything from where you need to be in this very moment. Be in the truth of your heart. Let it be. Allow healing inward to come to you. Keep feeling and opening to the unknowns, and use your self-expression through mindfulness, movement, voice, and emotion.

There are no hard written rules when it comes to death and the loss of your child, and that will forever be a part of your lived life as you move forward with new experiences. You get to take your grief and heart and create with it in a new and different way. That is honoring yourself and your child of light. I can only promise you that when you move into communication and allow yourself to receive in-between worlds of energy that you do get to transform into another part of your own purpose in this reality. So remember not to waste your most beautiful time and creative force in the suffering, and open up to your grief. Let it move you into new places of self-discovery and the deepest love you can ever experience

I remember a child of light once told me the space that he was in was made out of rainbows of light and the air smelled sweet like fruit. That his presence was whole and the purity of love. He was truly okay and thriving and guiding his mother and family.

I remember a little girl was born still. Her mother was a lovely spirit herself and was ready to have her baby girl. The mother never expected that her daughter would die in her womb at 40 weeks. When her daughter was born in the hospital, the many who were with her in this birth received energy and insights. That being the doctor, nurses, and family. I was told when this little girl's eyes would meet others that this unlocked some kind of download for everyone. It gave them healing, even though her experience with her body became separate.

PRACTICES WITH SPIRIT BABY COMMUNICATION

Spirit Baby Communication Practice – Child of Eternal Light

- Find a quiet space and sit comfortably.

- Close your eyes, align your spine, and feel your whole body.

- Starting at the top of your head, you'll be moving your awareness slowly down. Check in with yourself first by saying hello to your head and neck. Farther down, say hello to your upper mid-body (chest), then to your breath and lungs, and onto your belly.

- Keep going downward into your lower back and hips saying hello. Then to your legs and feet.

- Let your body's check-in create an open space of ease and relaxation.

- Next, bring your attention to your heart and listen to your spiritual heart center.

- Allow your intention to sense your spirit baby is here now.

- Share a personal love statement from your heart and let this example guide you: *Hello my baby daughter or son, I am here for you. I love you. I trust our loving connections together.*

- I want you to imagine or sense and feel that you and your baby are in a Heart to Heart connection together. I want you to feel this beautiful rainbow light hugging both of you together.

- In that rainbow of light I want you to allow the love frequency to keep rising and rising with each breath that you take.

- When you feel complete after 10 to 20 minutes, then end your meditation with prayer or an intention of gratitude and love.

MEDITATION - AUDIO Version

Direct Link:

https://www.newearthchildren.com/meditationnotes-from-spiritbaby

QR Code:

CHAPTER ELEVEN

Abortion – Releasing Pregnancy and Heart Healing

"The spirit lights of aborted babies, as small as they may seem individually, collectively illuminate the deepest and darkest corners of fear. Whenever there is the fear of being found out, the lights of their spirits shine. Whenever there is guilt, shame, and regret, their silent lights can help to illuminate the way back to peace."

~ Hollister Rand, *I'm Not Dead, I'm Different: Kids and Spirit Teach Us about Living a Better Life on Earth*

I am sorry you have to experience termination/abortion and/or pregnancy release. It is not something to be taken lightly, and nobody really understands what happens when you feel it is your only option or necessary choice – whether for a health, mental wellness, financial, or genetic/medical issue. You are not alone. And I have supported many women, over the years, who were seeking conception into pregnancy after an earlier termination.

Termination is a highly sensitive area of discussion within cultures and communities. Pregnancy release has had a strong political and religious tie to it throughout history. I cannot speak for the women who have had to make such a life-altering and challenging decision and choice, but what I can say is that I hold you in the highest of compassion and love. I know more than anything, women in pre/post-abortion just want to be loved, held, and supported through it. I have met many women in their young years into their twenties who were not ready for motherhood and others, mothers already, who are not ready for more children. I have not met a woman who did not feel like it was an extremely difficult choice or devastating to the heart.

Letting go of pregnancy is not simple and easy. Many women have different belief systems put into place within their lives. The cultural and societal fears and judgments present many opinions that can be damaging and traumatic for women. This is especially true as they try to heal and create a new life and connection with the self and, oftentimes, a partner and family.

I have received so many questions throughout the years about abortion and spirit baby communication. They were asked by women who were ashamed, scared, and feeling guilty and afraid of punishment or rejection. Others contacted me because they could sense their baby, feel their baby, and wanted to know what it means and how to get forgiveness. My goal is to ease your heart and support your healing, whether you are in a pre- or post-abortion place in your life and ready to bring the healing of spirit communication into it.

What does spirit baby say about abortion?

Abortion will never be an easy experience because you are a conscious, mighty, creative agency that has a heart of extensive spirituality. Any kind of birth loss creates a temporary rift that gets remodeled in times of grief. Grief is going to be a piece of your experience within abortion, whether it is a wanted or an unwanted pregnancy. The grief experienced after abortion can be denied, stuffed away, hidden, and completely neglected, but it still exists. It is so crucial that your grief relationship is acknowledged after a loss, and that you can be taken care of in a loving space and be treated with respect and love for your personal process. The next best piece of advice is to know there is nothing to rush or any energy to misinterpret.

I feel that many women, before or after abortion, who come to spirit baby awareness and recognize spirit baby connections have a different spiritual open-hearted ability to heal better. Knowing that your baby is not mad or angry at you is supportive. That is because your spirit baby and you are on a journey together to understand who you are, who they are, and what they have brought to teach and guide you. It is a highly unique experience with no one-size-fits-all approach for you.

Now I want you to take your arms and wrap them around yourself. Take a moment of breath and heart. Receive that hug of tenderness and self-love. Understand that your baby loves you. Your baby says hello. It is time for you to create a relationship for you to heal those parts of your past for yourself and your spirit baby. You will not give energy to your self-created sufferings or self-abusive emotions. That is what you are NOT meant to do. Definitely don't do this alone either. Yet only you can bring that positive spirit baby and heart communication forward.

Your Mastery of Spirit Baby Communication Is Your Own

Your baby is LOVE. You are allowed to receive that love. You are allowed to ask for assistance. Ask your spirit baby to guide you, like in the other chapters, to help you discover what you both need. Yell it out loud, cry it out, or don't cry or yell at all. Express yourself and explore this through song, dance, journaling, therapy, counseling, and more. An abortion does not end the existence of your spirit baby or babies, only the body for now, and that may be temporary or not. You get to figure it out through your life, your own inner explorations, and by using spirit baby communication with it.

Is spirit baby okay? What happens after an abortion with spirit baby?

Spirit babies can easily stay within the energy of parents, especially families, through lineage until being born again or not being born at all to you personally. Sometimes a spirit baby can move within the family and that all depends on the healing that wants to happen.

I have had some say their spirit baby went to a friend's family to be born. I saw this with a woman who came looking to conceive without any birth loss, and I will call her Samantha. Samnatha had a very enthusiastic energy and love about her. She had a session to bring some insights to her lack of conception and struggle, while she was in preparation for it. She never had an abortion, but her spirit baby had me ask if her mother had an abortion – which was a surprise for us all. Her mother did have an abortion before Samantha. It was a very curious message. The spirit baby wanted Samantha to know this for her own healing. That Samantha had not caused a conception issue nor needed to hold this in her past. It was a hidden or subconscious story held by history, and we received this because it was time to let it go and move forward.

Not every abortion will end up with a spirit baby earthside someday. I met a woman who was a new hiking friend, who I will call Julie. Julie and I had tea, and as we sat together, I could not help but feel this boy spirit with her. I did not say anything because it was not my place to nor was she asking for a spirit baby reading. Weeks later, we hiked up another beautiful mountain trail on the other side of town, and I felt that boy again. Julie was 50 years old and not interested in ever having a child or children. On the hike, Julie shared that she had an abortion, and in that moment, I realized that a spirit baby boy was offering her some guidance and healing. Julie's conversation made me believe that she was not interested in bringing awareness to him or exploring that part of her heart. She wanted to believe he was a thought or past idea, but not a child in spirit. His energy would possibly remain with her until she is ready to acknowledge him in this life and move on, or wait until the reunion of the afterlife.

Many babies I meet in spirit that have experienced abortion are typically open and loving energies. Most are open for spiritual bonding toward higher levels of living, unless the baby is ignored or if you are not open or available for it. When the spirit baby is ignored through fear, then the spirit baby may work harder to get your attention in different psychic ways such as meditations, dreams, and/or other friends or family. It is optional to pretend to not feel or sense a connection or not to take advantage of the lesson and healing.

Spirit babies want their mothers and oftentimes fathers to be involved in healing. Each abortion experience is different and the reasons are different. What happens after your abortion is grief and that grief is a normal response to being human because a death has occurred. After we experience death, then grief comes. You cannot shut down your feelings and mind into thinking otherwise and that is a good thing! The grief felt is experienced differently for each and sometimes the initial shock brings emptiness, confusion, overwhelm, and/or other emotions that need noticing that can include relief and more.

How do I grieve when I am experiencing guilt and/or shame?

Please give energy and space to your emotions and feelings. Experience the pain of your sorrow, sadness, anger, disappointment, denial, guilt, and any other emotions. Your emotions are a compass that points you to a needed direction to be open with and address. You have a full range of emotions, and raising this into awareness will bring a deeper perspective of your abortion experience. You may have trauma, and this is normal because it is a physical, emotional, and spiritual experience.

The energy of abortion is its own journey, and I am here to teach self-love, forgiveness, and the cleansing of old patterns of self-suffering in order to uplift you into healing, empowerment, and transformation. I have met many women in the distress of shame, overwhelm, anger, sorrow, and fear. I have supported the unwinding of the women's hearts and spirit baby messages for a depth of healing power, regardless of reasons such as medical issues, not the right timing, an abusive relationship, life path, or an unsupportive partnership.

I have my own thoughts around terminating pregnancy and what happens in the body for the women and the energy of spirit baby. I will not and have not ever judged or held any negative emotions for a woman who is or has gone through an abortion. I genuinely hold love and compassion for you, and most can feel it. In my many sessions, women are fearful that I will judge them because this is what happens in the world. I truly do not. I bring love and empathy.

If you experienced the inner guidance to let go of your pregnancy through a safe way of medications, procedures, or natural remedies, then you know this is your path. Healing is here now, no matter what you think and believe. It is valuable to healing to understand that you have a spirit baby connected with you. That light-bodied being in spirit is with you to share and teach, and for you to love and learn. It is not always a solo choice.

I want to explain more.

I am going to share some thoughts on the idea of choice. The notion that the "choice" of abortion is one-sided is untrue. What if your baby agreed to it? What if the trauma you hold inside was a part of a healing path? The trauma is not alone the actions of abortion but something already living in the feminine field of you, and your energy is responding to that energy. It is not always a conscious choice. The sacred calling into womanhood is not everyone's same experience. It is bravery, it is power, it is creation, it is light, and so much more!

How can I prepare my body, mind, and spirit pre-abortion?

Perhaps you are in the pre-abortion stage, and you're trying to figure out if this is the best step for you and what to expect from going through an abortion. I want to encourage you to create a ritual or ceremony before you go for the abortion and after to ease your heart. A ritual would include some kind of honoring of your own heart space and the releasing of this pregnancy, together with spirit baby communication.

Rituals & Ceremony for the Heart – Pre- & Post-Abortion

- Write a love letter to your spirit baby.
- Create a nature mandala outside with flowers, sticks, and leaves.
- Say prayers or intentions for the healing.
- Find a special music track for healing, calm, and ease
- Create a meditation that includes heart chanting or mantras.
- Do and/or receive an energy balance that includes using your Energy System/Chakras to ground and cleanse, like Reiki or other energy methods.
- Go to a crystal shop or metaphysical store, and buy something with your baby spirit.
- Create an altar that offers support with candles, pictures, and statues.
- Journal and write words like Love, Forgiveness, Kindness, Compassion, Bravery, Purity, and so on.

Remember in pre-abortion that there are going to be many different feelings and emotions. One time, during a particular session, I was supporting a woman who did meditations and more before the procedure. She was upset after her abortion because of the strong feelings she experienced. I told her, "Even though you are doing this for the betterment of everyone, that does not mean it will be without grief or other emotions to process after." She assumed she would not be sad or have big feelings.

I see all types of abortion or miscarriage as traumatic, and it leaves energy to work on after. The trauma can resolve and that depends on the experience and healing acquired before and after. It is very individual. I feel like we need to understand that after an abortion, a postpartum period occurs. That leads into a time to rehabilitate and regenerate the constitution of the cycling body. This needs space to be with and move into with ritual and ceremony.

How can I prepare my body, mind, and spirit post-abortion?

It is much like pre-abortion. There are many ways to prepare the body, mind, and spirit after abortion. It is very similar to pre-abortion in creating space for emotions, so the body can heal properly on a physical level, and be with the loss and grief. I suggest you create ritual and ceremony. Also, get into a supportive space for women, like a group or circle that gets you and your experience. It can be helpful to connect with others.

Joining others is deeply healing and a part of the journey. I was asked to create an abortion group online years ago and I did. There was a friend and Earth mother who suggested we collaborate. I actually loved the idea of supporting women, who are in pregnancy and post-abortion. Women need women to find their best selves, access their superpowers, and thrive with it.

Spirit baby communication, especially in abortion, can offer you an extremely deep healing, I believe. Your baby is listening, even if you feel like it is just you talking –whether it is in telepathy or feelings from your heart.

Review the chapters on spirit baby communication and styles to create your heart-healing, spirit-baby-communication practices.

When you are in spirit baby communication, you're bringing more energy to the acknowledgment of who you are and where you are now in this very moment. You are going to have a lot of different thoughts in your head, and you're going to also feel a lot of strong emotions. Keep encouraging yourself to access your feelings. If it feels unsafe to be in your emotions, then I highly advise reaching out to a therapist, counselor, and/or healer. I have seen that women in pre- and post-abortion who get counseling and therapy support are able to accelerate the processing of all the feelings and release them into the forgiveness and love that waits ahead of you.

Spirit Baby Communication Practice – Pre- & Post-Abortion Messages of Love

- Find a quiet space and sit comfortably.

- Close your eyes, align your spine, and feel your whole body.

- Starting at the top of your head, you'll be moving your awareness slowly down. Check in with yourself first by saying hello to your head and neck. Farther down, say hello to your upper mid-body (chest), then to your breath and lungs, and onto your belly.

- Keep going downward into your lower back and hips saying hello. Then to your legs and feet.

- Let your body's check-in create an open space of ease and relaxation.

- Next, bring your attention to your heart and listen to your spiritual heart center.

- Allow your intention to sense your spirit baby is here now.

- Share a personal love statement from your heart and let this example guide you: *Hello my baby being, I am here. I am grateful for you. I love you.*

- Allow yourself to experience the energy of forgiveness and to experience a release and surrender of judgment, criticism, or shame.

- Your spirit baby communication connection is all about your healing.

- Your spirit baby wants to share with you something really powerful and they're going to share with you a word that has everything to do with this journey of release.

- I want you to take that word and really see it as an energy form. That your baby is working towards your healing with that specific statement or phrase or word.

- Allow yourself to take time here to be in your body to feel the expression and connection of your spirit baby connection.

- When you feel complete after 10 to 20 minutes, then end your meditation with prayer or an intention of gratitude and love.

MEDITATION - AUDIO Version

Direct Link:
https://www.newearthchildren.com/meditationnotes-from-spiritbaby

QR Code:

CHAPTER TWELVE

Newborn Spiritual Care – Parenthood after Spirit Baby Communication

"During fetal development, radiance circuits are the first energy circuit to appear in the embryo, before meridians. Babies see, feel, sense, and know energy when they are born, and they see the energies that surround you."

~ Diane S. Speier, *Life After Birth: A Parent's Holistic Guide for Thriving in the Fourth Trimester*

Congratulations, you are an open-hearted spiritual mother and/or father who is ready for your new earth child and/or earth children. Care for the causes of humanity begins with you. You, as a conscious and awakened being of soul/spirit, who is on a mission with the purpose of bringing your child/children to Earth for a beautiful, fun, joyous, and creative family experience.

Your spirit baby communication journey was only the beginning of expanding Who You Are and what comes next. Your spiritual parenting is attachment parenting, intuitive parenting, and/or natural parenting. "Attachment parenting" involves the emotional bond between parent/caretaker and child. You want the bond to be strong and consistent. The bond is everything to the biological and spiritual wellness to the life of a newborn. If you want to go deeper into the science and psychology theory, it is best explained by researching *John Bowlby's* and *Mary Ainsworth's* work in this area of attachment.

Newborn care is just like spirit baby communication. Even though your baby has a growing infant body, that does not mean that the child's spirit/soul has changed. In our sessions, many have noticed that spirit baby is just like their earthchild in personality with quirks and little things remembered from before. It is super fun and intuitive to recall and experience a relationship together, learning and discovering other new things. And you will be using your instincts to connect to the nature of caring for your baby, along with instructions from others who have been there as parents and pass along basic and traditional knowledge.

Newborn Spiritual Care into Spiritual Parenthood

Ways to keep developing and achieving your way forward...

- Be a parent of Integrity.
- Be a parent with great Empathy.
- Be a parent with Unconditional Love.
- Allow the nature of a relationship that has attachment parenting.
- Always communicate and talk about feelings. (Remember, baby feels you.)
- Learn how to follow your natural mothering instincts.
- Always be open when you need deeper support.

- Allow imperfections and surrender controlling fears.
- Keep building your love relationship with your child.
- Always give and receive love and forgiveness.
- Your energy and self-regulation will be reflected in your child/children.
- Take responsibility for yourself and try to always practice presence.
- Be adventurous and bold with laughing and seeing the humor in parenting.

Your child has come to you to share their love and connection, to grow with you, and to show you their own purpose. But your biggest challenge as a parent is not only this unique soul being. Parenting is also about showing who you are. Your inner child will be reflected in your parenting style. I'm not going to go deeply into all kinds of parenting styles because there are way too many. I will say that parents have to do the best that they can do. Be honest, communicate, listen, allow for mistakes, and repair what's wrong with forgiveness, healing, and most of all love.

The New Earth Child Sometimes Needs Healing

Through child sessions and readings, I have supported many children who are born. That means I work with children in infancy, toddlerhood, and beyond. They can have issues and need support. On occasion, it's just about a curious parent wanting to know who their child is and how to support them in fulfilling their purpose.

I begin with a conversation with the mother or parent of the child in a quiet space where I can look at their energy field. Then I share information from the psychic intuitive space for additional support. I like to support challenging areas with babies and children who need insights that nobody can seem to offer or figure out. I have worked with children in neonatal intensive care units (NICUs) or traumatic emergency experiences with heart defects, other issues, and life-threatening accidents. I've also supported children who have unknown immune issues, allergies, and diagnoses that need another perspective. I am often met with relief, gratitude, and a welcoming of a holistic energetic remedy.

When I'm working with a child's energy in the psychic intuitive space using my "medical intuitive" abilities, I'm looking at the energy body in a certain way. I am getting whatever information is needed from the physical, emotional, mental, and spiritual bodies. I can give that to the parents, which typically is the mother, grandmother, or friend. The ultimate goal is to get any visuals and sensations into a form of communication and conversation so the next steps of the journey can be supportive and healing.

I supported a woman in pregnancy, and she went on to give birth to her sweet little baby. Later on, she came to me with a second child after her pregnancy. This child was born with heart issues. He spent a lot of time in the hospital, in and out for months, with multiple surgeries. This sweetest and kindest mother needed support, and not just for herself. She wanted to know what her son was feeling and experiencing regarding what was happening. Her biggest fear was that he would not make it. I am going to call him Jona

Jona was the sweetest little being, and he shared many things. This included how he felt in his physical body with the procedures, even the colors in the space, a nurse he mentioned by name that he liked, and many other things. His mother felt that even though she may not have been able to be there all the time physically, energetically she could still share in the healing for him and with him. To see how he was doing. It was great considering his situation of multiple surgeries and unknown issues that came up unexpectedly. He made it through with many impossible moments with much hope and faith. Some would say he was a miracle child.

More Sensitive Children - The Support They Deserve

I have met many children into teens and mothers seeking insights about their sensitive and bright energies that can be challenging. Most seek to understand who their daughter or son is so that they can be supported, for who they are and who they are becoming. I remember a toddler girl, who I will call Daisy, she had a fire-like spirit and energy about her. She needed to be cared for in her own way and with firm boundaries and flexibility.

Another child I met, who will call Lee, was holding onto his birth experience and it caused a chronic autoimmune diagnosis at 3 years old. Nobody could find the cause or reason. It was unresolved foundational emotional trauma that began at the birth. After birth the energy showed up through physical issues and healing was needed to move forward. It was not just about the child, but the mother and father. It was a family experience and together they can get support through different holistic methods like homeopathy, play therapy, cranio sacral, and other gentle body-mind techniques.

The children that come for my support tend to be more empathic, and energy sensitive aware children or many would consider Starseed or Indigo. A Starseed child is defined in many ways, but the common definition is that Starseeds are on an intergalactic mission to bring peace and love to humanity and earth through the "Golden Age." The Golden Age being a new time upon earth that is about bringing peace and love and harmony. These children I would agree do need extra support and do hold a big responsibility. It is not easy for the parent, but understanding who your child is and has come to be will support everyone the best towards guiding their personal mission.

Over all, children are all unique in soul, body, and purpose. All children offer a gift and I have the pleasure of seeing that energy in great clarity and how it is used and how it can be balanced. The world is challenging and changing and children are the grace of our future. Even in the positive beautiful times they can also acquire anxieties and phobias. It isn't simple and it can go deeper into the family lineage and birth experience. It can be hard to know and identify origins of issues at times, but practitioners and other medical and or healers, and psychological support try their best.

The Future Is Positive -Hearts Can Be Held High

The intuitive, psychic, sensitive child is the future of all children, who continue to grow and show up for their mission. It is a profound and powerful time to be in creation with life. Your child gets to teach and guide you as you do with them. What is next to come will be seen and experienced. It is an important time to save and heal the future of humanity, especially through our own heart path that is leading us forward and not backward.

I do feel that we are in a new era of Spirit Baby Communication working with the New Earth Children. So I want to leave you with a note to remember. Remember who you are on your deepest level and not the you that has the name and the personality. I'm referring to the you who is really just the essence of energy, light, and spirit. Remember that you were once a spirit baby being yourself, and now you are expanding into bringing forth your own child or children into this world.

Your parenting manual and or instructions are imprinted into your heart. You have everything you need inside you. Remember that always. I promise you that spirit babies and earth bodied children, who are your sons and daughters in between worlds or upon earth, are in communication with you. Energy always speaks first. They're sharing with you all the time, and they're offering you healing, teaching, and guidance. You are learning, and you are breaking down old thoughts and ideas to receive what it means to be parents for a New Earth. So keep expanding, exploring, and discovering who you are in spirit baby communication relationship and with your New Earth child. Promise yourself forgiveness and surrender and always remind yourself of freedom and love.

It is and has always been love that keeps everything in working universal order and connected to who you are. You are ready. You are capable. You are purity. You are light. You are Star.

CONCLUSION

Thank you for opening up your heart and allowing your mind to explore freedom and new ways to thrive within intuition, conscious conception, and into birth. Parenthood is the most challenging, chaotic, rewarding, and incredible experience to venture into next to finding partnership and love. Your child or children will guide you in so many ways that will keep you learning and evolving.

No matter where you are on this planet and spiritual path – whether it's conception, miscarriage healing, pregnancy, birth loss healing, and/or creating a loving, healing birth for you and baby – you are in the right place and where you need to be on your healing journey. Remind yourself that you get to connect with your intuitive psychic self in the most authentic and humbling ways. I really want to promote that and encourage you to always remember who you are and who you continue to become. Keep being in alignment with your own heart. You are ready. You are whole. I send you so much love!!!

REFERENCES

Australian Aboriginal Conception Beliefs by Francesca Merlan

https://www.jstor.org/stable/2803097?seq=1

Australian Aboriginal Conception Beliefs Revisited

Inuit Pregnancy & Conception Beliefs by Dan Ketchum

Inuhttps://classroom.synonym.com/inuit-pregnancy-conception-beliefs-11481.htmlit Pregnancy & Conception Beliefs - Synonym-

ABOUT THE AUTHOR

Kelly Ann Meehan, MA is a healing visionary, published author, birth advocate, and a holistic mother to her sons Rain and Forest. Her loving services with sessions and programs focus on spirit baby communication in conception, energetic fertility healing, medical intuition, pre-birth connection in pregnancy, and sacred grief support in all areas of birth loss (miscarriage, stillbirth, & termination). Kelly understands how to listen to the unseen and deeply felt world of spirit baby and more.

Kelly holds a BA, Psychology & Masters in Clinical Psychology with an emphasis in Somatic Psychology. A majority of her experience is in the field of children and families working in Attachment Parenting for her MFTI hours. As an MFT Intern she helped lead groups on attachment parenting and family psychotherapy, and was a parent and toddler group leader/coordinator. For years she worked as an infant development specialist in early intervention and has led parent and toddler groups in the community of the Palisades, Santa Monica, and South Los Angeles. Always wanting to learn more, Kelly has additional training in Energy Based and Somatic Based modalities such as: Reiki I, Cranio Sacral Therapy, Infant Massage Instruction/ Parent Education, and Yoga with Mini Yogis (children's yoga teaching certification.) She has completed the training for the Advanced level Integrative Energy Therapy (IET) I, II, and III before Masters level. She is a trained Death Midwife with Sacred Crossings and completed her 4 week training with Apprenticeship with Sorrow with Francis Weller.

Kelly is the host and creator of SPIRIT BABY RADIO Podcast since 2016. The only one of its kind that speaks about Spirit Baby. The intention is to bring conversations about soul baby communication, the before life of conception, the afterlife within birth loss, future parenting, New Earth Children, psychic awareness, intuition, the space of dreams, energetic healing, and so much more!

She has been in the media on birth related and spiritual podcasts and radio shows as a guest expert, being invited and attending over 40 online global summits with topics such as: fertility, pregnancy, grief, and spirituality. She has been featured in Blogs, magazines, and articles. She has been on a TV Show (Nighttime Prime) Nick MOMS.

Instagram: @spiritbabymedium

Facebook: Spirit Baby Medium/Medical Intuitive

Facebook: SPIRIT BABIES: Conscious Conception, Intuitive Pregnancy, & Motherhood

Facebook: The After Life of Spirit Baby- Healing, Connections, & Love

Twitter: @SPIRITBABYRADIO

YouTube: https://www.youtube.com/@spiritbabycommunication

WEBSITES https://www.newearthchildren.com/ / www.spiritbabymedium.com

https://www.spiritbabyacademy.com

EMAIL spiritbbabymedium@gmail.com

SERVICES https://www.newearthchildren.com/services

SPIRIT BABY RADIO https://www.newearthchildren.com/spirit-baby-radio

PROGRAMS https://www.newearthchildren.com/programs-workshops

PRODUCTS https://www.newearthchildren.com/spirit-baby-oracle-cards

Printed in Great Britain
by Amazon

61535128R00131